You Can Manage Your Time

You Can Manage Your Time

Lucy MacDonald

Rosen
YA
New York

This edition published in 2018 by
The Rosen Publishing Group, Inc.
29 East 21st Street
New York, NY 10010

Additional end matter copyright © 2018 by The Rosen Publishing Group, Inc.

Library of Congress Cataloging-in-Publication Data

Names: MacDonald, Lucy, 1953– author.
Title: You can manage your time / by Lucy MacDonald.
Description: New York, NY : Rosen Publishing, [2018] | Series: Be your best self |
Audience: Grade level: 7–10. | Includes bibliographical references and index.
Identifiers: LCCN 2017001894 | ISBN 9781538380024 (library bound : alk. paper)
Subjects: LCSH: Time management—Juvenile literature.
Classification: LCC HD69.T54 M3235 2017 | DDC 650.1/1—dc23
LC record available at https://lccn.loc.gov/2017001894

Manufactured in China

Photo Credits: Cover Maridav/Shutterstock.com; interior pages design NottomanV1/
Shutterstock.com

CONTENTS

INTRODUCTION

We've all been there. Running through the house looking for lost car keys, late for an appointment, thinking about the mess we're leaving behind, wondering when we will have time to drop off the dry cleaning, worrying that our current school project will not get done on time, angry that the person in front of us is moving too slowly. Hurry up, hurry up, we tell ourselves and those around us. The whole world is in our way. We feel stressed, upset, and resentful.

From the time we get up in the morning until we put our heads on the pillow at the end of the day, we think about what we have to do, and we worry about what's not getting done. We wake up in the middle of the night worrying about when we will find the time we need to complete the never-ending list of "To Dos." If something goes off schedule we just give up, despairing that we will ever be able to catch up.

If this sounds like you, you are not alone. We are living in a period of the time-starved; we are rushed with no end in sight. People are exhausted and overwhelmed, with no time for personal conversations, for taking a leisurely walk, for waiting patiently for family members to finish their dinner.

Having enough time is the luxury item of the moment. Today men and women—and even children—all around the world are experiencing increasing levels of time stress. This chronic stress is linked to poor physical and psychological health.

We all have the same twenty-four hours in the daily time bank. Time is the constant, so what needs to change are the choices that we make about how we use our time. Managing time is about making decisions concerning how you want to live your life. You have the life you have because of the decisions you make regarding how you spend your time. If you want a different life, you must make different decisions. If you are not convinced about this, look at the successful people you know and pay attention to how they spend their time.

My own life is an example of how managing time has enabled someone to achieve their goals. My earliest recollection of the importance of time management goes back to when I was five years old and my youngest brother, Robbie, was born. The long-awaited day when he was coming home arrived, and I so wanted to be part of the welcoming party. My father told me to hurry up and get ready. Excited, I took immense care and a long time to choose the perfect outfit for this important event—only to discover that the welcoming party had left without me. I was devastated. This incident made such an impression on me that to this date, I hate being late for anything.

My mother was also instrumental in teaching me how to manage my time. Despite having five children, she was employed in an era when most mothers did not work outside the home. She was able to keep things running fairly smoothly by maintaining a routine and being an expert in delegation, enlisting all five of us to help with daily chores.

I've acquired my time-management skills through trial and error. Each stage of my life has presented different challenges when it comes to time, and I have had to make adjustments. I learned basic time management skills when I became the mother of four children whose ages range over ten years from oldest to youngest. I quickly realized that unless I kept a very firm grip on the daily schedule, the family descended into chaos. I also discovered that it was essential to put into practice my mother's one and only piece of parenting advice: "When you need time for yourself, take it, because no one will come and offer it to you."

It wasn't until I returned to college at the age of thirty-nine, when my children were aged between eight and eighteen, that my time-management skills became finely honed. I attended college for six years—winter, spring, summer, and fall—and completed a BA in psychology and a masters in education and counseling psychology. In order to graduate I used all the main time-management techniques outlined in this book. I had a vision of what I wanted to accomplish. I set myself goals. I created a plan for each semester, and I lived according to a weekly and daily schedule. I learned how to avoid procrastination and how to deal with disruptions and time-wasters. I used my daily planner as a road map to achieve my goals—much the same as I do today.

After graduation I started a private counseling practice and seminar business, and once again my ability to manage my time effectively was, and is, a tremendous advantage. As I am a self-employed businesswoman, time is the framework within which I earn a living—a poor grasp of time would be reflected on my business balance sheet.

However, don't get the impression that I always manage my time well. That's simply not the case. I continue to be challenged by new situations, but I am motivated to get back on track because I believe that by wasting my time I am wasting my life. Whenever I hit difficulties, I am able to renew my commitment to use my time wisely by revisiting my life purpose and goals.

Time is an extremely precious resource, and managing it well can help you to achieve your goals and your dreams. *You Can Manage Time Better* is a straightforward, step-by-step guide that can be of benefit to anyone, anywhere—from a child to a retired person, and at school, at home, or in the workplace.

I hope that you will use this book to set yourself free: free from the chronic hurriedness of everyday living, free from the fear of wasting time, and free from the tyranny of having too much to do and not enough time in which to do it.

Ultimately, how you spend your time is how you live your life—so spend it wisely.

UNDERSTANDING TIME

I wish I had more time," is a common complaint. Although we can't increase the number of hours in the day, we can decide what we are going to do with them. The first step to gaining control of your life is to understand what effective time management is and how it will help you to reduce time-related stress.

In this chapter you will discover everything you need to know to start managing your time. You will learn different ways to track how you spend your time and how to focus your energies on the most productive and fulfilling activities. You can use the hurry zone quiz to get an idea of your level of "hurry sickness," then follow the practical suggestions to help you slow down and enjoy life a little more.

FORMS OF TIME

If I were to stop you in the street and ask you what time it is, chances are you would look at your wristwatch and tell me. But what if I were to ask you "What is time?" If you are not able to answer readily, you are in good company. The concept of time has tested the greatest thinkers throughout history.

In the seventeenth century Isaac Newton proposed the idea that time is absolute—a universal, steady process that everyone everywhere experiences in the same way. Albert Einstein challenged Newton's idea of time with his general theory of relativity—that time is relative, dependent upon how fast we are traveling.

Another way to try to understand time is to take a brief look at horology, the study of time measurement. Throughout history civilizations observed the stars, the cycle of the seasons and the movement of day into night, devising ingenious ways to track the passage of time. The earliest Egyptian calendars were based on the moon's cycles and evolved into a 365-day calendar around 4300 BCE. Starting in 1582 the Gregorian calendar was adopted by most of the West and is the most commonly used civil calendar today.

What, then, is time? If no one asks me, I know what it is. If I wish to explain it to him who asks, I do not know.

St. Augustine
(354–386)

Originating in the eleventh century, the hourglass was used to gauge everything, from the speed of a ship to the length of a preacher's sermon. In the 1300s mechanical clocks using weights or springs were built in Europe. The advent of the mechanical clock marked the shift from observing the passage of time to providing a precise calibration. Clocks were further refined with the development of the pendulum clock in the 1600s. With each generation of clocks, the measurement of time became more accurate. The development of the wristwatch made the measurement of time portable, while the mass production of watches made it widely accessible. Today we have the cesium fountain atomic clock that keeps almost perfect time. Off by only a second every twenty million years, this clock is far more precise than most of us will ever require in our day-to-day lives!

HOW WE EXPERIENCE TIME

The ancient Greeks conceptualized time as either *chronos* or *kyros*. Chronos is clock time measured in seconds, minutes, and hours, and it is the root of words such as "chronology" and "chronological." Kyros is timelessness, living in the here and now, synchronicity and carpe diem—seizing the moment. Chronos and kyros represent quantity and quality, which reflect what our struggle with time is all about. While chronos is fixed at an objective rate, kyros varies considerably because it is subjective and can be a positive or negative experience. To most people forty-five minutes spent in the dentist's chair will feel longer than the same period of time spent reading a fascinating book.

How can we experience more positive kyros time and less chronos? Doing one thing at a time, refusing to live an over-scheduled life, and making time for the important people and activities in our lives are key ways to help us balance the quantity and the quality of our time.

WHAT IS TIME MANAGEMENT?

Time management is really a misnomer. We can't actually manage time because it moves on regardless of what we do or don't do. The objective is to take control of the time that we do have, so that we can fulfill our needs and responsibilities. You want to make sure that your intended use of time equals your actual time use. Chronically mismanaging your time can leave you feeling hurried and harried. Time management can be described more accurately as self-management.

We can all make better choices about what we do with our time. Think of someone you know who is a good time manager. How would you describe them? Organized, productive, competent, happy, calm? That is what managing time can do for you.

Day-to-day time management is about finding a system that helps you to gain more control over your twenty-four-hour day so that you can balance roles, spending your time doing the things you want to do and have to do. There are many time-management systems, from simple paper planners to state-of-the-art computers and smartphones. Your might prefer one system or another, depending on your circumstances and stage of life, so don't be afraid to let go of a method that no longer works for you and experiment with another approach as your needs change.

There is no one, right way to manage time. Your approach depends on what is important to you: this book will help you identify these values and goals, in both the long and short term. But regardless of what type of time-management system you choose, the key is to use it!

Successful people recognize that time management is crucial to help them to reach their goals, both personal and professional. Learning to manage your time effectively and efficiently is an important life tool that can help you at home and at work to achieve whatever is important to you.

MISCONCEPTIONS ABOUT TIME MANAGEMENT

Perhaps you've never tried managing your time because you don't think you have the time to do so. Perhaps you've tried managing your time, but wound up using a system that was awkward and time-consuming. The truth is that time management does require an initial investment of your time—to draw up a plan, to get organized, and to determine how you wish to spend your time. But once you've laid the groundwork, you need less than ten minutes per day to put your plan into action.

Although the best time-management plans are often the simplest, time management is not necessarily mere common sense. For example, are you truly achieving your goals? What? No goals? Then identifying your goals would be a great place to start. Are you spending your time wisely or is your time account on the verge of being overdrawn? A plan is required along with the daily self-management or discipline to use that plan. Have you ever heard anyone say, "Time management takes away the edge I get from working under pressure?" There is a difference between having enough pressure to motivate ourselves to get things done and being in a panic because we're in danger of missing the deadline. Procrastinating is never a good thing, and the chronic stress of having to work feverishly on tasks to make up for lost time as the due date approaches is simply unhealthy.

If you are worried that learning to manage your time well is going to make you inflexible and take all the fun and spontaneity out of your life, think again. Structuring your time means including time to go to the movies, or take a walk, or read that bestseller. Want more time and more spontaneity? Block off a few hours each month with no set plan or goal and see where the free time takes you.

THE BENEFITS OF TIME MANAGEMENT

By managing your time you can improve your quality of life. Imagine waking up knowing that you will be able to accomplish the day's tasks with a minimum of stress. Who wouldn't want that?

Reduce stress and anxiety. Much of our daily stress is related to the time crunch: too much to do in too little time. Structuring your time will help relieve chronic stress, which, over weeks, months, and years, becomes a slippery slope toward burnout and depression. Reduce your stress and anxiety levels by including some relaxation in your schedule.

Increase personal satisfaction. When was the last time you had that "job-well-done" feeling? Not using our time effectively leaves us feeling dissatisfied with ourselves, resulting in us putting ourselves down and thinking negatively. Schedule enough time to get the job done by adding some buffer time to take into account unforeseen interruptions and delays.

You are in control of your life. This is your life and you get only one go (as far as I know). Taking control of how you spend your time is permitting yourself to live the life you choose. Make a three-column list: "Must Do," "Should Do," and "Would Like to Do." Your "Must Do" list includes non-negotiable things, such as making a living and looking after your children. Evaluate your "Should Do" list and see how many "Should Dos" you could stop doing. Now add some "Would Like to Dos" into your schedule.

Create work–life balance. Scheduling your time helps you create balance between your work and personal life. Making an appointment with yourself emphasizes that personal time is just as important as work time.

Be more productive. Organizing your time helps you to accomplish more in the allotted time because you are able to focus on the job at hand without worrying that you should be doing something else.

Achieve more of what is important to you. Using a good time-management system helps you not only to get things done but also allows you to examine why you are doing certain chores/jobs and thus focus on what is meaningful and personally rewarding to you.

Start by doing what is necessary; then do what is possible; and suddenly you are doing the impossible.

St. Francis of Assisi

MAP YOUR TIME

Exercise One
Some days it can feel like you don't accomplish very much. To discover exactly what you do with your time, try this exercise, which will help you to list all your various activities, tasks, and responsibilities over the course of one month.

1. *Taking a sheet of paper and a pen, jot down the various roles you play in your life—for example: husband, father, daughter, employee, volunteer, friend, and so on.*

2. *Now take another sheet of paper and divide it into columns, writing one role at the top of each. Under each role list the activities associated with it. For example, under "father" you might have "reading the children a bedtime story" and "taking the boys to soccer practice." Make sure to include socializing, such as meeting with friends, as this also requires time.*

3. *Update your list daily, but if this is not practical, do it at least twice a week.*

4. *After a month review the list and assign a number from one to five to each activity, task, and responsibility, one being most important and five the least.*

5. *Analyze your results. How many ones do you have? How much time do you spend doing them? And how many fives? How much time do you spend doing them?*

6. *Starting with your least-important activities, tasks, and responsibilities, assess whether they are all really necessary. What would happen if you stopped doing them? This will help you weed out unimportant activities and give you more time to spend doing important things.*

TIME URGENCY

Everyone, it seems, is in a hurry. Wherever we go we can witness the effects of "hurry sickness": people getting upset because they have to wait in line, motorists honking horns because the driver in front of them is not going fast enough. You might succumb to "hurry sickness" if: you regularly find that you are short of time; you have too much to do so you do everything as quickly as possible; or, a delay of any kind upsets you.

In the 1950s, doctors Meyer Friedman and Ray Rosenman coined the term "hurry sickness" while studying personality types. As a result they defined the "type A personality," which is characterized by impatience, hostility, competitiveness, tension, and aggression.

Expanding on the work of Freidman and Rosenman, Dr. Li Jing L. Yan zeroed in on a yype A behavior pattern that has three main features: time urgency/impatience, hostility, and competitive drive. In 2002 Dr. Li Jing L. Yan found that of the three thousand men and women he studied, those who spent their twenties hurrying from one thing to another and feeling impatient were twice as likely to have high blood pressure fifteen years later than the people who took things at a slower pace. High blood pressure is an important risk factor for developing heart disease and/or having a stroke.

Living in a state of chronic time stress has a poor effect on your health. Feeling constantly pressured for time can weaken your immune system; cause muscle pain, insomnia, and headaches; and increase your risk of depression and anxiety. Stress as a result of time urgency and hostility can decrease the supply of blood to the muscles of the heart, and studies have shown that these time-pressure episodes can be a precursor to a heart attack.

As with many problems, we can modify and manage the problem of time urgency. Take time to do activities

THE RELAXED PERSONALITY

Friedman and Rosenman also developed a personality profile called the type B personality. Type B people are able to work without becoming anxious and agitated, be patient with delays, and relax without feeling guilty. Here are some ways to develop type B characteristics in yourself:

- Concentrate on speaking slowly and pause briefly between sentences—people will experience you as more thoughtful and less aggressive.
- Participate in activities involving slow movement, such as tai chi or drawing, to help you appreciate unhurried, deliberate action.
- Don't take delays personally. Delays are part of life and most often have nothing to do with us (unless, of course, we've not allowed ourselves enough time to get things done in the first place).

that require you to slow down. Visit an art gallery; listen to someone without interrupting them; do only one thing at a time; or take up meditation. Practice patience when waiting in line—the proverbial "counting to ten" technique is quick and easy to use in such situations. Of course, it is important to make sure that you leave yourself enough time to get your errands done in the first place. Estimate how long each task will take you and then factor in extra time for delays, such as traffic jams. Walk instead of driving whenever possible—walking is good exercise and it will help to release stress.

Abdominal breathing using your diaphragm is another great way to slow down. To get a sense of abdominal breathing, try placing your right hand on your abdomen and your left hand on your chest. Inhale slowly through your nose, allowing your abdomen to expand first. Your right hand should move outward as you breathe in and your left hand should stay relatively still. Now practice it without using your hands. This is an excellent way for you to reduce stress in almost any situation. You might like to try this the next time you have to wait in line. This is also a wonderful relaxation technique to teach to children.

Though I am always in haste, I am never in a hurry.

John Wesley
(1703-91)

FIND YOUR HURRY ZONE

Exercise Two

Take the hurry zone quiz to discover if you are in the green, yellow, or red hurry zone. Answer each question and award yourself points according to the following scale: 0 = never 1 = not often 2 = most of the time 3 = always.

Then add up your total score and discover which zone you are in.

- *I walk fast.*
- *I talk fast.*
- *I'm impatient when people speak slowly.*
- *I interrupt people when they speak.*
- *I like being first in line.*
- *I'm impatient if I have to wait in line or in traffic.*
- *I eat my meals quickly and often don't take time to enjoy what I'm eating.*
- *I do more than one thing at a time.*
- *I'm fidgety.*
- *I get my work done quickly.*
- *I get impatient with office machinery.*
- *I charge around when I'm shopping and often forget things in the process.*

Your score
Green Zone = 0 to 12
You are in the "no hurry" zone. But if you scored any 2s or 3s, look for ways to slow yourself down in such situations.

Yellow Zone = 13 to 24
Proceed with caution! Try to become hurry-savvy; that is, allow more time to do things and make an effort to slow down.

Red Zone = 25 or more
Stop! You are in hurry overload and you can't continue without serious consequences to your well-being. You must take stock and make yourself slow down.

THE PARETO PRINCIPLE

Have you ever noticed that approximately 80 percent of decisions come from 20 percent of meeting time; that 80 percent of the phone calls you make are to 20 percent of the people in your life; and so on. In time management the Pareto Principle (named after its inventor Vilfredo Pareto), also known as the 80/20 rule, is the idea that 20 percent of time and effort generates 80 percent of results. Of course, the corollary is also true: 20 percent of results take up 80 percent of time and effort.

The quality management expert J.M. Juran described the 20 percent of time and effort as the "vital few" and the 80 percent as the "trivial or useful many." When you are functioning in the "trivial many" (the 80 percent zone), you may complain about how little time you have, be doing tasks that you are not interested in or not particularly good at, or be doing things that are not connected to either your short- or long-term goals. You are functioning in the "vital few" (the 20 percent zone) when your interest is high, you are good at what you are doing, your creativity is being put to good use, and you are contributing to your short- and long-term goals.

Focusing on the 20 percent that matters ,the 80/20 rule helps us to shift the focus away from being busy for its own sake to concentrating on results. Use a list of your "vital few" activities (see Exercise Three, below) to remind yourself when you get sidetracked by "trivial-many" items, or when there is a crisis. After a crisis use the list to make sure that you don't waste any precious time in the 80 percent zone.

KEEP A TIME-USE DIARY

Exercise Three
This exercise is specifically designed to help you evaluate where your 80/20 time split falls by recording and assessing the relative importance of every activity you perform over a seven-day period. You will need a diary or small notebook, a pen, and a sheet of paper.

1. *Taking your diary or notebook and pen, mark out your waking time for the following seven days in fifteen-minute periods.*

2. *Each evening fill in how you spent your time that day. Make sure that you include everything, no matter how trivial it might seem. Do this until you have a record for the entire week.*

3. *Review where your time went. Take the sheet of paper and draw two columns. Name one "Personal" and the other "Work" and allocate your week's activities accordingly. (Whether you work in an office, from home, or are a full-time parent—you work.)*

4. *Next, decide which activities fall into the 80 percent zone. Then analyze which activities are in the 20 percent zone. For example, if you sell gift baskets from home but spend two hours per day filing, are those two hours developing your business? No. So such filing is a "trivial-many" activity. A "vital-few" work-related activity might be contacting customers to ensure that they were satisfied with their order.*

5. *Once you have a clear idea of where your time is going, resolve to focus more on the important "vital-few" activities and begin to cut down on the less productive "trivial-many" things that you do.*

WHAT'S STOPPING YOU?

Some of the biggest and most common obstacles to managing time efficiently are procrastination (putting things off, and perhaps never doing them at all), perfectionism, fear of failure, fear of success, and workaholicism. These obstacles all have one thing in common —they originate in our thoughts, beliefs, and our self-concept.

In this chapter you will explore how to stop the cycle of procrastination and how to break the drive for perfection, which holds you back from accomplishing new things. You can also take a quiz to find out if you are working too hard. You will be given all the tools you need to change your negative thinking and to discover what is holding you back from becoming an expert time manager.

PROCRASTINATION

It is 3 a.m. and Janet is sitting at her desk, staring into space. She is feeling very anxious because she needs to come up with some clever and innovative ideas for the company's latest sales drive, and she has to present them to her boss tomorrow morning. She knew three weeks ago that the deadline was tomorrow, yet she didn't start working on the project until yesterday. Was she too busy? Perhaps the task was too difficult for her or she wasn't briefed properly? None of the above: Janet is struggling with procrastination, and it's causing her a great deal of stress.

Procrastination—from the Latin *pro cras* meaning "for tomorrow"—means to defer a task until the last moment, or even to fail to do it at all. At a simple level, procrastination can result in missed deadlines, but it can also leave us feeling guilty, inadequate, self-loathing, and even depressed.

If people feel so bad because they leave things to the last minute, why do they do it? Here are some of the reasons why we procrastinate.

Fear of failure. "I just know I can't do a good job of this. Better not to do it at all than to show them that I can't do it."

Fear of success. "If I make a good job of this project, they'll continue to expect more and more from me." Or, "I don't deserve praise—recognition makes me feel uncomfortable."

Negative self-beliefs. If you tell yourself over and over again "I'm not good at this," you will put off the anxiety-producing task.

Being too busy. "I am much too busy to get anything else done."

Being disorganized. "I need to get myself organized before I can write that report."

Poor planning and time management. "I should not have

spent so much time with my friends over the weekend when I knew that I had this job to do."

Getting easily frustrated. "I just can't stand it when I try to work and it doesn't go smoothly or easily. I quit."

Depression. "There's no point even trying to do this. What's the use?"

Reflect on the price you are paying for procrastinating: anxiety, depression, and stress. Also, be realistic about what it has cost you in grades, employment opportunities, or career advancement and the toll it has taken on your relationships.

Now resolve to do something about it. The earlier in the cycle you can stop yourself, the easier it will be to get back on track. Then, break down the task into small, manageable steps. Write a schedule, setting a date by which each step will be completed. Now comes the crunch—getting started. This is often the biggest hurdle, but start you must. After you complete a step, give yourself a little reward. Then, following your schedule, start on the next one. As you complete each step you will gain in confidence, and before you know it, you will finished. Congratulate yourself!

STOP PROCRASTINATING NOW

Exercise Four

If you are currently delaying doing something that you know needs to get done, here is a way to talk yourself into meeting that important deadline.

THE CYCLE OF PROCRASTINATION

Between tasks we start the procrastination cycle by thinking "Next time, I'll start earlier." Then, when we have our next task, we think "I'll start soon." Anxiety builds as we begin an internal chain of thought along the lines of:

- What will happen if I don't start?
- I'm doing everything except what I should be doing.
- I can't enjoy doing anything else while this is waiting to be done.
- Why didn't I start sooner?
- What if someone finds out that I'm in this mess?

But the procrastinator thinks, "There's still time for me to get it done." However, then self-criticism often sets in and they lose confidence, asking "Do I get the job done or do I abandon ship?" Having failed to complete the task and feeling very negative, the procrastinator vows never to put things off again. But after the memory of the anxiety has faded, the cycle begins again.

1. Write down the task that you are avoiding. "Study more" is too vague; something more specific, such as "Write essay on Shakespeare's sonnets," is much better.
2. Ask yourself why you are avoiding it. Don't you like the task? Are you afraid that you can't do it well? Do

you feel you are too disorganized? If you are having difficulty discovering why you procrastinate, ask a friend or colleague the reasons why they might put things off.

3. *List reasons why delaying might benefit you. For example, you can do other things that you prefer instead; you don't actually have to get down to work; you don't have to face anxieties about the task; and so on.*

4. *List reasons why delaying might hurt you. For example, you won't get a good exam grade; or your children will be too embarrassed to have their friends over if you continue to avoid cleaning the house.*

5. *Think positively about yourself and the task before you. Break the task down into smaller, more manageable chunks, and set yourself mini deadlines by which you need to have completed each part of the task. Aim for completion, not perfection.*

6. *Ask a friend or colleague to help you by making you accountable to them. Tell them the date by which the task has to be completed and get them to check on your progress from time to time.*

PERFECTIONISM

When we have a task to do, most of us strive to do a good job. However, for some people, this is not enough—they want to do a perfect job. Perfectionists live in a world of self-imposed, unrealistic standards and expectations that cause them to strive continually for the unobtainable. They don't tolerate mistakes, and they become bogged down in the smallest details, often starting over again and again in a bid to get the job done absolutely right.

In time management, perfectionism and procrastination are two sides of the same coin because both prevent us from using our time wisely and completing the task. A perfectionist seldom accomplishes anything that is acceptable the first time around. They may delay starting a task because they know that it will take a huge amount of energy and they will become frustrated, angry, and anxious as time passes.

Perfectionism often starts in childhood as a desire to please others. Gifted children can struggle with the high standards imposed by adults and take on these standards as their own. They may mistakenly internalize the message that their value is equal to their performance. The child wants to please their parents and teachers, and over time their desire to please others turns into a fear of rejection. Often motivated more by fear than the desire to succeed, the perfectionist may avoid new situations or refuse a job promotion because they are afraid that they cannot perform to their own high standards.

The perfectionist lives by the rule of the "should:" I should be perfect and everything I do should be perfect; I shouldn't make mistakes; I should always give 150 percent regardless of the circumstances; I shouldn't attempt to do things if I know ahead of time that they won't be perfect.

Being a perfectionist can be a lonely experience. Low self-esteem and lack of confidence are obstacles that perfectionists struggle with. Unwilling to try new things for fear that they can't do them well, the perfectionist may become stuck in rigid thinking about what they can and cannot do. Perfectionists are at risk of pessimistic thinking and depression. All-or-nothing thinking is a forerunner to pessimism and depression in the perfectionist's world. Anything less than 100 percent success is a total failure. "If I can't do it perfectly, I won't do it at all."

OVERCOMING PERFECTIONISM

Accept that making mistakes is a human trait. You will learn more about yourself through failure than success, but nothing is a complete failure if you've learned something.

Strive for excellence instead of perfection. Block out the time required, do the preparation, get the job done in the time allotted, and feel good about it. Use the Pareto

Principle to help you learn where to put your time and energy. In this case 20 percent of your effort produces 80 percent of the quality. Doing an adequate or satisfactory job (the 80 percent) is much better than getting nothing done at all.

Learn to differentiate between doing something right and doing the right thing by asking yourself if the details that you are fussing over are important to the overall project. Give yourself a reasonable schedule and stick to it. Use a small alarm clock or timer to remind you when the time is up. Then force yourself to move on to the next task. Factor in time at the end to review and tweak, but set a time limit on that as well. Be patient with yourself as you practice being imperfect.

Perfectionism is a trap that is worth escaping—when you do, you will like yourself more, enjoy the process of doing things rather than focus solely on the result, expand your repertoire of skills, and, most important, you will be able to let go of the stress and anxiety that are intrinsic to being a perfectionist.

CREATE A COLLAGE OF YOUR ASPIRATIONS

Exercise Five
What would you do if you knew that you didn't have to do it perfectly? This exercise helps you discover what you have always wanted to try but were afraid to, because your inner perfectionist is holding you back.

1. *Assemble the following: a collection of different types of magazines (lifestyle, travel, business, gardening, and so on), a large sheet of art paper, a pair of scissors, and some glue.*

2. *Block off one hour of time, play some of your favorite music, light a scented candle, and take a moment to relax. Flip through the magazines, one page at a time, and continually ask yourself the question, "What would I like to do if I knew I didn't have to do it perfectly?"*

3. *Follow your impulse and tear out any pictures that represent something you'd like to try but haven't because of your need to be perfect in all things. Don't censor yourself or question your abilities. Just follow your intuition.*

4. *After about thirty minutes, use the scissors to trim the images and paste them onto the art paper to create a collage.*

5. *Reserve the last fifteen minutes to think about which activity you would like to try most. How would you begin? For example, say you'd like to make over your garden but have been intimidated by your own high standards and the size of the task. You might start by planting a small window box. Whatever you choose, the pressure is off when you no longer need to be perfect.*

FEAR OF FAILURE

No one likes to fail at anything and a fear of failure is one of the most common anxieties we face. Everyone has doubts about their abilities from time to time, which can cause them to hesitate to try something new or something they know they are not particularly good at. A fear of failure is linked with a fear of being criticized or rejected, but not all fears are bad—our innate survival instinct, which is based on fear, protects us from harm and warns us of danger. However, fear becomes a problem when it limits our capabilities and diminishes our quality of life.

The fear of failure can spiral into a vicious cycle. The anticipation of the worst-case scenario leaves you feeling anxious and stressed. You withdraw from the task at hand and/or from others because you feel embarrassed and don't want to ask for help. You abandon what you are doing, or keep putting it off, or perhaps you never even start. Your self-confidence plummets and you generally feel bad about yourself, thinking, "I'm a loser, I can't do anything." You feel like a failure in all areas of life; your anxiety increases.

Yet people who accomplish their goals know that failure is a natural by-product of trying. If you don't try, you will certainly never fail—but you won't succeed either.

Ask yourself what exactly you are afraid of. Being judged? Looking silly? The possibility that friends or colleagues won't like you? Is there any evidence to support these fears? What's the worst that can happen if someone judges you? Often, once we have accepted what the worst outcome could be, our fears lessen and we feel more positive about trying.

Try not to let your emotions control what you are going to do and when you are going to do it. Take action first and the good feelings will follow. Similarly, don't wait until you get in the right mood before starting; instead, just get going—your mood will improve because you are doing something and you will feel better about yourself because you are trying. Avoid undermining yourself and asking yourself "what if" questions, such as: "What if I can't do it well?" and "What if I fail?" This will only drain your confidence. Focus on your effort—that is the most important part—and congratulate yourself for trying.

Develop persistence. Follow the advice of the American humorist Josh Billings (1818–85): "Be like a postage stamp—stick to one thing until you get there." Keep trying and when you get anxious or frustrated give yourself ten more minutes to work on the task and then take a short break. Then, return to work with renewed determination to see the task through.

Inevitably, everyone experiences failure at some time or another, and when you do you will realize that missing a deadline or not managing to complete a task is not as terrible as you had thought—it doesn't mean you lack character and it doesn't reflect on your value as a person. Instead of chastising yourself, try to use the experience as an opportunity to grow and develop.

It can also help to review a situation where you failed to complete something because you were afraid of failing. Identify where you got stuck. Was it before you started the task, after you started it, or toward the end? Why do you think you stopped when you did?

What may be done at any time will be done at no time.

Scottish proverb

Were you unprepared to do a certain aspect of the task? Did it take longer than you thought and you panicked at the idea of running out of time? And so on. Once you have some answers, you can approach your next task differently so that the fear of failure does not prevent you from completing the job.

Finally, watch your thoughts. Be aware of your internal dialogue when things go wrong. "It didn't work out" is quite different from saying "I am a failure." Changing your perspective and reframing the failure as a temporary setback will allow you to learn from the experience and move on.

FEAR OF SUCCESS

While the fear of failure is the fear of making mistakes and looking foolish, the fear of success is the fear of achievement and the recognition that success brings. People who struggle with the fear of success often do not understand why they have problems making decisions, lack motivation to achieve their goals, and are chronic underachievers. If they do complete something successfully, they denigrate their achievements, put themselves down, and say that it was just a stroke of luck.

Those who fear success are masters of self-sabotage. They set things up to fail: they hand in the report late or incomplete, or they don't turn up for their creative writing workshop even though their work is highly regarded by the teacher. But why? Perhaps being successful does not fit with their self-concept. They view themselves as undeserving of success.

How can the fear of success sabotage effective time management? Self-sabotaging your time-management efforts can occur in subtle ways: not preparing a schedule when you know that this is the best way for you to operate; not using your calendar even though you carry it around with you; letting people interrupt you and take up your valuable time when you are trying to finish a project; or waiting until the end of the day when your energy is low to work on important projects.

It's a good idea to analyze what would be different in your life if you stopped sabotaging yourself and became successful. What are the pros and cons of success? There must be some benefits from self-sabotage or you wouldn't be doing it. Perhaps you don't want to deal with the consequences—such as promotion or moving house—that success might bring? Once you pinpoint why you are sabotaging yourself, you can start to address the problem.

Another way to push past your fears to success is to define your goals, both long- and short-term. While the fear of success is in the present, your goals are future-oriented. Use them to remind yourself why you need to overcome your fears.

A little positive brainwashing can also go a long way to helping you overcome a fear of success. Repeat to yourself, "I deserve to be successful," at least ten times a day. Also, write out this positive affirmation on small, adhesive notes and put them in places where you often see them, such as on your bedroom mirror, on your computer monitor, on the dashboard of your car, and so on.

FIND YOUR OWN DEFINITION OF SUCCESS

Exercise Six
How will you know when you are successful? What does being successful mean? This exercise will help you to discover your own personal definition. You will need a paper plate or a sheet of paper with a circle drawn on it and a pen.

   1. Divide the paper plate or circle into segments representing the areas of life that are important to you (see diagram below). Label each segment and mark on the numbers as shown. Now indicate your satisfaction with each area of your life on a scale from 0 to 10 (where 0 = not satisfied at all and 10 = completely satisfied). Draw a line across each segment at the appropriate point and shade in the area produced.

2. *Join up the points on the segment lines. Chances are, you are closer to your definition of success in some areas than others. Reflect on how you have achieved success in these areas.*

3. *In the segments where you rated your level of success as low, answer the question: "How will I know when I have achieved success in this area?" For example, in Physical, your answer might be: "When I can run a half marathon."*

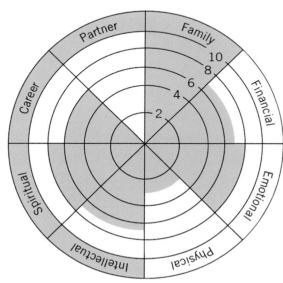

WORKAHOLISM

Being a workaholic is a socially acceptable addiction—no one looks down on hard workers: we encourage and reward them. There is nothing wrong with loving your studying, feeling satisfied when you have put in a long day, and going the extra mile to make sure a project is completed on time. The difference between a hard worker and a workaholic is control. The hard worker is in control of when and how hard they work, and there is a balance between work and the rest of their lives. The workaholic, on the other hand, feels anxious when not working, finds it almost impossible to relax, and sometimes resents time spent with family and friends. The key indicator that a person is out of control and a workaholic is the bad state of their personal relationships. Spouses and children often suffer most because their husband/wife/ father/mother is spending so little time at home. Workaholism can be an important factor in divorce, and children of a workaholic parent often complain about the lack of time spent together.

Workaholics can be found in virtually every profession and work setting: doctors, lawyers, carpenters, teachers, social workers, artists—no occupation is exempt. People in professions that use hourly billing, or work according to a corporate culture that rewards those who put in extra-long hours, or entrepreneurs and the self-employed are especially at risk.

Work addiction takes both a physical and a mental toll. Stress caused by burning the candle at both ends can result in many symptoms, such as: high blood pressure, anxiety, skin rashes, a depressed immune system, insomnia, bouts of anger, impatience, nausea, and back and joint pain. And if the workaholic does not slow down and learn to enjoy time away from work, he or she is at risk of burnout.

Although burnout is not recognized as a medical condition, it can be very debilitating. Burnout related to work addiction is a type of depression that develops as a response to work-related stress—in this case caused by spending too much time at work. It develops over years and is characterized by physical exhaustion, sadness or depression, taking longer to complete work responsibilities, shame that you can't work as hard as you used to, poor concentration, and an inability to make decisions. Many workaholics refuse to acknowledge what is happening until their symptoms are so severe that they are physically unable to address the problem. At that point, we need rest and recovery. Burnout often forces us to reassess who we are in relation to work, why we do a particular kind of work, and what needs to change so that we can find a better balance between work and the rest of our lives. Returning to work gradually, with a renewed sense of purpose and a more flexible attitude, will help us to become happier and healthier.

The road back from workaholism and burnout can sometimes feel slow and painful, but it can be done. A good start is to let go of the guilt and anxiety of not working 24/7. Remind yourself that you are a better employer/colleague/entrepreneur/student if you take time to relax and revitalize yourself. You will be more efficient, creative, and productive.

Make sure that you give the important people in your life a chunk of your prime time. Stop giving your family and friends the leftover time at the end of the day and on the weekends and spend some time with them when you are in top form. Perhaps you could schedule some fun time for a Saturday morning when you would normally go to work, or set up (and keep) a date night once a month with your partner or with friends.

Take time to take care of your physical health. Being in good physical shape has many well-known benefits, but for the workaholic there is an additional one: It requires taking time away from work. Schedule time to run, to go to the gym, or to use exercise equipment at home—whatever you can do to help you get, and stay, in shape. Exercise helps to manage anxiety and stress and produces mood-enhancing endorphins. Exercising with others, such as your siblings or friends, will give you the added bonus of rebuilding your relationships.

As you incorporate changes into your work routine and work less hours, be aware that you may experience withdrawal symptoms. You might find yourself feeling down, especially if you liked the adrenaline rush associated with a fast-paced, all-consuming work life. You might also feel agitated and impatient. These feelings are normal and common when lessening the grip of the amount of time and energy that your work consumes.

Time management is not a method for you to work harder and longer. Effective time management incorporates all of the areas of your life from work to family to leisure.

ASSESS YOUR ATTITUDE TO WORK

Exercise Seven
This exercise is adapted from *How do I Know if I am a Workaholic?* published by Workaholics Anonymous. Answer the following questions with a simple "true" or "false" response:

- *I get more excited about my work than my family or anything else.*
- *I take work with me on vacation.*
- *Work is the activity I like to do best and talk about most.*
- *I work more than fifty-five hours per week.*
- *My family and/or friends do not expect me to be*

on time.

- *I believe it is okay to work long hours if I love what I am doing.*
- *I get impatient with people who have other priorities besides work.*
- *I am afraid that if I don't work extra hard I will lose my job or be a failure.*
- *I worry about the future even when things are going very well.*
- *I get irritated when people ask me to stop doing my work in order to do something else.*
- *My family complains about the amount of hours I work and that I am rarely home.*
- *I think about work most of the time: while driving, when falling asleep, when I wake up during the night, when others are talking to me.*
- *I work or read work-related material during meals.*

The more "true" answers you have given, the closer you are to being a workaholic. An awareness that you might have a problem is the first step toward changing. If you feel that you might need professional help, contact an organization such as Workaholics Anonymous or seek advice from a mental health professional.

LEARN TO SET LIMITS

Exercise Eight

There are only twenty-four hours in a day and it is neither healthy nor desirable to spend more than one third of this time working. This exercise will teach you how to cut back on long working hours and regain a balance in your life.

1. *First you need to find out exactly how you are spending your time, so get yourself a notebook and pen. For the next two weeks you are going to record everything you do. Each evening write down what you did that day and how long each thing took. List everything, including everyday activities such as sleeping, eating, and bathing.*

2. *Analyze your time record, concentrating on the time you spent working over and above your required hours (in most jobs a maximum of eight hours per day). Look for ways gradually to reduce the extra hours.*

3. *Start by making small changes. (If you try to make too many changes too quickly they won't last.) For example, try finishing work half an hour earlier each day until you leave at the designated time. Or, take fifteen minutes every lunchtime to go for a walk.*

4. *Learn to say "no," both to yourself and to others who*

make demands on your time. Don't add anything to your schedule without removing something that requires the same amount of time and energy.

5. *Find a mentor to support you in your quest to reach a better work-life balance, someone you can trust: your partner, a friend, or even a counselor. Set up a system whereby they can alert you, or you can go to them, if you veer offtrack.*

QUALITY TIME

Do you know where you are going in your life? If you don't, how will you know when you arrive? You need a map to give you direction, motivation, and a time frame. How you spend your time is a reflection of what is important to you. Identifying your values will give you an understanding of what you are trying to accomplish with your life.

This chapter provides you with the necessary guidelines for writing a personal statement of purpose, or a "mission statement." It shows you how to set goals and gives suggestions about how to reach a balance between your work life and your personal life.

WHAT IS IMPORTANT TO YOU?

If someone were to follow you around for a week and record how you spend your time, would they be able to extrapolate what is important to you? Are you happy with the way you spend your time? At the end of most days, do you feel satisfied that you've spent the bulk of your time on the things that are important to you?

Time management is more than creating "To Do" lists using detailed diaries or studying time-use grids. Organizing your time isn't a way in which to get everything done, because that is simply impossible. If you approach life with an attitude of, "If I hurry up, if I work harder, if I work faster, I will be able to accomplish it all," you will end up feeling frustrated and discouraged, not to mention exhausted. What is possible is to accomplish the things that are most vital to your personal and professional well-being.

Let's now look at the Pyramid Principle and the Priority Principle—two ways to evaluate your time and to make sure that you are using your time doing what is most important to you.

THE PYRAMID PRINCIPLE

Charles R. Hobbs was influential in the 1970s and 1980s for moving time management away from techniques to increase productivity and toward developing a personal time-management approach grounded in core values. Hobbs felt that it was important to have a cohesive system that incorporated individual values, goals, and daily planning. This he did by creating what he called a "productivity pyramid." The first step in building a productivity pyramid is to define your values and write a general action statement about each—for example "Show compassion" or "Have faith in others." These Hobbs called the "unifying principles." You then use these unifying principles as a basis from which to formulate your long-term goals. From your long-term goals you set intermediate ones, and then base your daily goals on your intermediate goals. The pyramid is thus formed with your unifying principles at the base, your long-term goals in the next layer, your intermediate goals above that, and your daily goals at the top. This fits in with Hobbs' philosophy that any time-management system that you are actually going to use, must involve a synthesis between what you believe and what you do.

In *The Seven Habits of Highly Successful People,* Stephen Covey proposes that we sometimes go through a personal evolution of four "generations" of time management. Each generation builds on the next and becomes more effective and useful.

According to Covey most people who are interested in learning about time management use the "get organized" approach (first generation) that runs on reminders and "To Do" lists. There is no indication of priorities, no specific time allotted to specific tasks, and what they don't get done today, they put on tomorrow's list.

The second generation of time management is focused on planning and preparation. Calendars and agendas or diaries are the main tools we use; people set goals, make plans, schedule events. Typically, the only things that they schedule are work-related items, medical appointments, meetings with teachers, and so on. The schedule rules, and it does not tend to include the time we need to maintain personal relationships and to develop personal goals.

The third generation moves beyond planning and preparing and adds prioritizing and controlling. People functioning in this level of time management spend time articulating values and priorities. They divide goals into the short- and long-term, based on their own values. They use planners and organizers (paper or electronic), and often use highly detailed forms for planning their day. According to Covey what is missing at this level is the concept of spending time on what is actually most important.

Covey outlines the need for a fourth generation of management that moves beyond managing time to managing yourself and your life. It includes all the strengths of the previous generations and adds a quality-of-life component. It helps us to create and maintain meaningful relationships and peace of mind and engenders confidence that not only are we doing what matters most, we are doing it well.

THE PRIORITY PRINCIPLE

Value-based time management requires an understanding of what our personal and professional priorities are and our making time-use choices based on those priorities.

Charles R. Hobbs and Stephen Covey determined that our time use can be divided into four categories: 1. Important/Not Urgent; 2. Important/Urgent; 3. Not Important/Urgent; and 4. Not Important/Not Urgent.

THE FOUR CATEGORIES OF TIME USE

Category 1: Important and Not Urgent—Priority Principle
- Managing your time as an extension of your values and priorities
- Being able to focus on what you are doing without the fear that you should be doing something else
- Including time for relationships
- Examples: balancing work and personal time; scheduling time for relaxation, physical fitness, personal growth, and development.

Category 2: Important and Urgent —Crisis Management
- Giving your immediate attention and dropping everything else
- Examples: medical emergencies, deadlines, family or relationship crises

Category 3: Not Important and Urgent—Distractions as Denial
- Responding immediately to all distractions and interruptions; attending all meetings
- Examples: answering all emails and phone calls as they come in, regardless of who they are from; going out for dinner three or four nights a week with friends/colleagues

Category 4: Not Important and Not Urgent—Busy with the "Trivial Many"
- Spending your time on things that make little or no contribution to your quality of life
- Examples: playing card games on your computer; doing work-related activities, such as filing, that don't help to

build your career or your business; answering personal phone calls when you are working at home; allowing friends or family to drop in and distract you when you are working in a home-based business

Never leave until tomorrow that which can be done today.

Benjamin Franklin
(1706-90)

WHAT DO OTHER PEOPLE VALUE?

Think of five people you know who you particularly respect and admire, and arrange to interview them. In order to access as wide a variety of perspectives as possible, choose individuals from a range of ages (perhaps including a grandparent and a teenager), and diverse backgrounds, levels of education, professions, and so on.

Ask each interviewee to list the five values that they hold most important and adhere to in order to live a good life. Then find out why their chosen values are so important to them. Use the information gleaned from the interviews as a starting point to help you to determine your own values. The objective is to focus on creating a life that is based on the foundation of Category 1 principles, to learn to be an effective Category 2 crisis manager, and to avoid useless distractions (Category 3), and being busy for the sake of being busy (Category 4).

Living your life and using your time based on your principles and values will help you to accomplish your life goals, and create order in and balance between the different areas of your life. You will be in control of your life and, because you are managing your time effectively, you will have many fewer crises to deal with. Take a pen and a sheet of paper, and divide it into four sections: top left, Important/Not Urgent; top right, Important/Urgent; bottom left, Not Important/Urgent; and bottom right, Not Important/Not Urgent.

Now discover which category you are currently in. Take your calendar or agenda (or rely on your memory, if you must) and allocate a month's worth of your activities among the four categories, according to the criteria described opposite. The next step is one of assessment and reflection. Ask yourself: Which category was I in most of the time? How much time did I spend doing activities that were Important and Not Urgent? This should show you clearly whether or not you are spending your time wisely and focused on priority activities.

WHAT ARE YOUR VALUES?

To make the shift to living with your priorities in mind, you first have to determine what your priorities and values are. Your values are the beliefs that reflect your definition of a meaningful life—they drive your behavior. You can use your definition of success from chapter 2 (see Exercise Six) as a basis for determining your values.

Once you have ascertained exactly what your values are, the task of allocating your time becomes easier. As you learn to live your life and take charge of your time based on your values, you become sensitized to the good feelings that emerge as a result. Conversely, you will experience psychological discomfort when you spent time on unimportant tasks. If you find yourself doing this often, you need to reassess what you are doing and why and then make the necessary adjustments to get your value-based time management approach back on track.

IDENTIFY YOUR VALUES

Exercise Nine
Imagine that you have been asked to divulge to future generations the secret of living a meaningful life. You first need to compile a list of core values that you feel are essential to you personally, and which reflect what you consider to be most worth upholding and defending.

1. *Taking a sheet of paper and a pen, list all the values that matter to you down the left-hand side in a column. These might include: integrity; honesty; intimacy; friendship; family happiness; comfortable living; hard work; learning; physical and mental health; spirituality; personal growth; and independence or autonomy. Try to narrow down the list to your ten most important values.*

2. *Write a time-related statement of principle next to each value. For example, if friendship features on your list, you might put, "I will plan and schedule time to spend with friends." Or for personal growth, "Each year I will take one course that will help me to develop into a well-rounded human being." Keep the completed list and statements in your agenda and read them every day to inspire you.*

3. *Review your list and statements on an ongoing basis. Circumstances change, and so will the relative importance of some of your values. For example, if you become a parent, family happiness will probably become more important than independence. Hone your list and statements so that they give a full and accurate reflection of your current values.*

THE PURPOSE OF YOUR LIFE

People can be divided into the "haves" and the "have-nots." But I am not talking about their abundance or lack of financial success, being with or without the perfect partner, having that envied career, or putting a career on hold while you focus on raising children. There are those who have a definite sense of purpose; others who simply seem to wander aimlessly throughout their lives without any rhyme or reason. Some people who appear on the surface to have it all, in reality have a poor quality of life because they have no idea what their life purpose is—they are just putting in time.

Living your life purpose is at the heart of who you are —the very essence of your being. Living a purposeful life provides you with a sense of direction and mission. When you know what your life purpose is, you start every day with that in mind and plan accordingly; it shapes how you think, what you do, how you spend your time, and how you approach life. Your life purpose is not your job, or your roles (daughter/son, mother/father, and so on). These are vehicles through which you deliver your purpose. Your life purpose comes from within, from your values, and it should infuse you with joy and contentment.

Knowing what your life purpose is creates within you a desire to live with passion. This passion fuels your daily activities. When you are living purposefully you feel connected to a greater whole; you have an understanding that your purpose is part of a greater scheme of things, however you choose to define that.

The more we do, the more we can do; the more busy we are, the more leisure we have.

William Hazlitt
(1778–1830)

Writing a personal statement of purpose or "mission statement," will clarify the direction you should take in life. It will help you to stay focused when your enthusiasm wanes and at any time when you end up using your precious time on inconsequential trivia. Your mission statement is also a useful measure, on a monthly or yearly basis, of where you have been, where you are now, and where you are headed.

Once you have a clear idea of what your life purpose is, write it down. You will be able to use your statement of purpose as a guide in making both small and large decisions, such as which university to attend whether or not you need to move house or job;,and whether you should pursue a particular business venture.

A statement of purpose prepares you for stability in a world of constant change. The ever-changing nature of work, leisure (or lack of it), family, and social interactions has a tremendous impact on our daily lives. Having a statement of purpose can be a constant in your life while all

MAKE YOUR GOALS

Whether short-term or long-term, well-formulated goals are SMART. That is:

Specific – What you wish to accomplish, precisely detailed.
Measurable – Possible to assess in terms of progress.
Attainable – Within reach given your circumstances.
Realistic – Within your personal capability.
Time-lined – Possible to accomplish by a certain date.

Let's use the goal of physical fitness as an example.

Specific – Complete a half-marathon.
Measurable – Keep a weekly running log.
Attainable – Already a recreational runner.
Realistic – Eight months to train.
Time-lined – Entered for the half-marathon on September 17.

It is important to review your progress regularly and make the necessary adjustments so that your goals become a reality.

things around you are in flux.

Each one of us has a unique purpose. If you do not fulfill your life purpose the world is forever deprived of what you have to offer.

CREATING GOALS BASED ON YOUR VALUES

It is a good idea to write down your goals, as people who do so are more likely to accomplish them than people who don't. You can use your list of values (Exercise Nine) or your personal mission statement (Exercise Ten) to help you.

Start by making a list of what you want to accomplish this year. Then put the goals in order of importance. Starting with the most important goal, work out what steps you would need to take to accomplish it. For example, say that you want to improve your education. You will need to find the right course. Would an evening class be best, or can you talk to your employer and arrange to work fewer hours so that you can attend in the day? How will it affect your other commitments, such as looking after your children? Will there be financial implications? If so, do you need to set aside some money beforehand? Do you have to apply for the course by a certain time? And so on.

Think about each of the goals on your list in the same way, and break down each one into small steps that you can gradually achieve.

WRITE YOUR PERSONAL "MISSION STATEMENT"

Exercise Ten
Your life purpose = your passion + its benefit to others.
Once you determine your life purpose, you can encapsulate it in a personal mission statement.

This will always inspire you and remind you of what is important in your life.

1. *Let's start with your passion. It could be anything— from singing opera to DIY to bungee jumping. If you are unsure what it is, first take another look at the list of values you created in Exercise Nine. Now ask yourself the following questions and write down your answers. What do my friends and family ask my advice about? Do my friends see me as having expertise in a specific area? When I enter a bookstore, do I always gravitate to a specific section like gardening, physical fitness, or travel?*

2. *Next, consider who will benefit from your passion. Are you interested in sharing it with a specific group or profession, such as seniors, dentists, or single parents, or with people in general? Finally, how will others benefit? For example, if your passion is showing others how to find their work–life balance, a possible benefit will be that they get to enjoy more time with their children.*

3. *Look at your answers and then write a clear and concise mission statement, based on the following sentence stems:*
   - *My passion is ...*
   - *The main beneficiaries of my sharing of this passion will be ...*

LEAVE YOUR OWN LEGACY

Exercise Eleven
Use this exercise to help you envision the kind of life you want to lead and to help you to put in place some long-term goals.

1. *Imagine that you are listening in to your family and friends eulogizing at your funeral. What would you hope they would say about your legacy—the contribution you made to your family, your friends, and the community?*

2. *Be as specific as possible when formulating your personal legacy.*

For example:
3. *Once you have written your personal legacy, you can think about ways to turn this into a reality. For example, if you want to be remembered as a helpful neighbor, what do you need to do to become one? Perhaps you can set aside one Saturday per month on which to do errands for the elderly couple who live across from you. Write down on a sheet of paper for each "I would like to be remembered as ... " statement at least one goal that you can incorporate into your agenda or planner as a reminder.*

4. *Take your agenda and schedule your life-affirming goals over a six-month period. Remind yourself that every time you reach one of them, you are building your legacy.*

I would like to be remembered as:

- *A partner who ...*
- *A parent who ...*
- *A son/daughter who ...*
- *A sister/brother who ...*
- *A person who ... (fill in the blank) in my community*
- *A co-worker who ...*
- *A neighbor who ...*

TIME TO PLAN

We can remedy many of our poor time management habits through good planning. Choosing a planner is an important first step and you can find one that suits your lifestyle, whether you are a student, or a professional, or you are at home parenting full-time. Planning, both short- and long-term, will give you peace of mind, a purpose in life, and a sense of accomplishment.

In this chapter you will learn the value of planning each day, as well as the advantages of planning ahead several years. You can also have fun creating a list of one hundred things you would like to do in your lifetime, and learn how to turn these dreams into a reality.

CHOOSING AND USING YOUR PLANNER

Once you have made a commitment to become a good time manager, the next step is to find the right time-management tool that will help you keep track of your goals, and schedule appointments, and provide you with easy access to important information.

There is no shortage of choices when it comes to planners, from calendars, paper and pencil planners, and agendas to computer-based software programs and smartphones. Planners are available for professionals, such as teachers, lawyers, and salespeople, and for specific-interest groups, such as gardeners and dog-lovers.

The biggest dilemma when choosing a time-management tool is which format to use—paper, computer, or smartphone. So let's consider the advantages and disadvantages of each in turn.

Paper planners come in a variety of sizes and colors, and cover either the calendar or the academic year. They generally show either a day, a week, or a month per page. If you are uncomfortable with technology, like to be able to view your week or month on one page, feel more secure using a paper planner, and prefer writing to using a keyboard, you will probably find that a paper planner is your best option.

The week- or month-at-a-glance feature is handy for people who like to see their week or month in one place. But if you need to schedule appointments on a daily basis, the daily-view planner with plenty of space to write down appointments is a good choice. Also consider the size of your handwriting—the bigger your writing, the bigger page size you will need. There are benefits to using a paper planner: there are no batteries to charge, it is low in cost compared to electronic versions, and you can use it pretty much anywhere, except when you are driving! The disadvantages of a paper planner include the limited capacity to store information, the need to transfer annually-recurring information, such as birthdays and anniversaries, and (unless you keep a duplicate copy) nowhere to back up the information—so if you lose it you are sunk!

Computer-based programs can be good tools to help you manage your time, particularly if you use a desk- or laptop computer most of the time (either for work or for personal use), you are comfortable using computer software, you like to be reminded of scheduled events visually or with a sound, and you like to be able to store more information than a paper planner can handle.

Almost anyone using a desk- or laptop computer will have a calendar and contact-management system as part of their email program. You can also opt to use software dedicated solely to time management. A computer-based system allows you to sort, store, and organize almost limitless amounts of information. You can set up the program to remind you—with a "popup" on your computer screen, along with a sound alert—of impending appointments, phone calls, and other items that you have scheduled. Coworkers, employers, or assistants can also access these calendars. The disadvantage with a desktop computer is that it isn't portable; and if something goes wrong and you lose your information, often it can be difficult or impossible to retrieve it, unless you have previously backed it up.

The third type of planner available is a smartphone. Smartphones have become one of the most popular and convenient ways to keep on time due to the vast amount of free apps available to download, from "To Do" list apps that have brought list-making into the internet era to apps that can track how you're making use of your digital time and monitoring your productivity. If you travel a fair amount, need something small and portable, and need to be able to sync information electronically between you and other colleagues' home/ work computers and time-management tools, a smartphone is probably your best bet. Smartphone's have most of the same advantages as computers and when you add to that their portability, you have the road-warrior's time-management dream. Although it can sometimes take longer to set up a smartphone and to find the right place in which to input your data compared to making a quick note in a paper planner, the advantage of being able to store vast amounts of information makes it infinitely superior. If you are prepared to keep the smartphone charged and back up your data, then this may be the right option for you.

Here are some other guidelines to keep in mind when selecting your planner:

- Choose one and only one planner, and use it everywhere and for everything that requires scheduling. Store all contacts, phone numbers, and schedules in one place.

- Keep your planner in the same place for easy access—perhaps near the phone or on your desk. Don't forget to take it with you when you head out the door.
- If you want to include your long- and short-term goals, choose a planner that allows you to record and track your progress.
- Don't become a slave to your time-management system. Creating extensive "To Do" lists (and lists of your lists), and scheduling everything down to the last minute, will take the joy out of life and will actually be counterproductive.
- Make sure that there is a good fit between the way you work and your time-management system. Adapt the system to fit your style and the type of work you do—your time-management system works for you, not the other way around.

Ordinary people think merely of spending time. Great people think of using it.

Anonymous

PLANNING YOUR WEEK

Planning your life one week at a time offers a convenient time frame within which to operate because it includes both work time and personal time. Weekly planning covers a manageable chunk of time and is a good way to approach the bigger picture of your life.

Choose a specific time to plan for the upcoming week. Some people choose the end of the workday on Friday; others choose Sunday evening. Setting up your weekly planning session in a specific location, such as your desk at home or at the office, will help you be consistent with your weekly planning. Remind yourself to set this time aside by marking it down in your planner.

Start by quickly reviewing your "mission statement" (Exercise Ten), your value statements (Exercise Nine), and your long-term and short-term goals. It will help you to stay on track if these are at the forefront of your mind as you plan your week. Then, review your previous week and measure your progress against your planned activities. Were you able to get your important activities done? If not, why not? This information will be particularly helpful as you become more proficient and accurate in scheduling your time on a weekly basis. Your next step is to focus on the coming week. What would you like to achieve this week? Are these expectations realistic? Don't try to do too many things or you will become frustrated, stressed, and exhausted. But equally, if you don't do enough, you will be bored and not accomplish very much. Gradually, you will get a feel for how much you can comfortably get done in one week.

HOW TO SCHEDULE

Planning on a weekly basis will help you move from crisis-management to a more proactive, goal-oriented, and realistic time frame.

- Schedule your priority tasks at the beginning of the week to ensure that you will have sufficient time to get them done.
- Be aware of deadlines. Make a habit of scheduling tasks to be completed ahead of the deadline date. This will give you a comfortable time cushion in which to deal with emergencies or unforeseen events.
- Overestimate rather than underestimate how long it will take you to complete a project. Doing this will help you to get your work finished even if you are faced with interruptions and delays, and it will also allow you to work in a more relaxed, less stressed manner.
- If you are calling a meeting, schedule a set time for the meeting to end.
- Make appointments back to back. If you have two appointments in the same building (or in your home office), give yourself only a five-minute break between them.
- Schedule your work as an appointment with yourself.

HOW LONG WILL IT TAKE?

If you are not quite sure how long it will take to get a certain task done, ask yourself the following questions:

- What do I need to do?
- What materials do I need? How long will it take to get them together?
- When will I do it?
- Can I do it all at once or will I divide it into smaller chunks of time?
- Can I do it by myself, or do I need help? If so, when will this be available?

After you've completed the task, assess if your estimate of the time required was close to the reality. If not, look at why not, and use that information next time you need to estimate how long something will take.

- If you must interrupt your scheduled task to take care of an emergency, be sure to reschedule your task for as soon as possible.
- Once you have scheduled your priorities you can fill in some of your schedule with other, less important activities.

ANALYZE YOUR TIME BUDGET

Exercise Twelve

How can you manage your weekly time budget if you are not sure how you are spending it? Use this exercise to help you to budget the number of hours in a week against the amount of time you need to get your work and activities done.

1. Taking a sheet of paper and a pen, draw two columns. Name the left-hand one "Activities" and the right-hand one "Hours spent." Under "Activities" list everything you did during the last week: sleeping, eating, working, commuting, doing chores and errands, socializing, watching TV, and so on. Don't leave anything out. Then, using your diary or the time record you made in Exercise Eight and bearing in mind that there are 168 hours in a week, write in the right-hand column how long you spent during the last week on each activity.

2. Total up the number of hours you spent on everything. Now subtract this figure from 168. Was there any time left over? Or were you in time deficit? (This is not as strange as it sounds, because sometimes we do more than one thing at a time.)

3. Analyze your results. If you had any free time left over, look at your lists of long- and short-term goals, and allocate some more time to achieving these. But if

you were in time deficit, you need to reexamine your time budget to find yourself more time to spend on important activities. You need time to sleep well, to eat healthily, and to work. But do you really need to watch TV? Can you find a better use for that time? Try reallocating your time, until you are back within your time budget. With deft "pruning" you can even find some free time.

YOUR DAILY SCHEDULE

Great time managers use three basic tools of daily planning: a master list, a "To Do" list, and a schedule of appointments and meetings. A master list is simply a running list of everything you have to get done, and it is kept separate from your "To Do" list. Your master list is not prioritized in any way: its purpose is simply to list your "To Dos" as they come up. Having a place to keep an ongoing list frees you from the worry of forgetting to do something important. You can then refer to your master list to create your daily "To Do" list.

A "To Do" list can help you to stay focused on the activities and priorities for a particular day. You are more likely to complete things if you have a list and write down your plans for the day. It makes your responsibilities appear more manageable and less overwhelming. Check your list mid-morning and again at lunchtime to make sure that you are getting your priorities done first. Make sure that the planner you are using, whether it is paper, computer, or handheld, allows you space to create and update your "To Do" list fairly easily.

Another suggestion to keep you focused and motivated on a daily basis is, first thing each morning, to pull out your list of short- and long-term goals and read them—you could even write them out again if you have time. This is a great way to keep them fresh and uppermost in your mind.

At the end of your work or school day, take five minutes to plan the next day. If you wait until the morning to plan that day, too many things could interrupt you and you might find yourself with no plan at all. The first step is to review any commitments that have specific start times and to check that you've allotted them sufficient time. Don't forget to include travel time to and from meetings if you are leaving home or your office, especially if you live in a big city where traffic jams and problems with public transportation can delay you.

Using your time-management planner and anything left over from today's "To Do" list, write down everything that you would like to accomplish tomorrow. Now that you have tomorrow's "To Do" list, remove as many tasks as possible. Ask yourself whether or not you, personally, have to do everything on the list. Are there any tasks that you can delegate to your partner/children/friend/colleague? If so, ask for their help.

Draw three columns on a sheet of paper with numbers down the left-hand side. Name the three columns "Must

Do," "Would Like to Do," and "Reschedule." Before you decide which tasks should go into which column, ask yourself the following questions about each task:

- Is it crucial that I do this task today?
- Can I reschedule this task without any penalty to myself?
- Does this task help me reach my weekly goal? My monthly goal?
- Can I eliminate this task without any penalty to myself?

Now divide the tasks on your "To Do" list among the three columns. Schedule your "Must Dos" first, then add in items from the "Would Like to Do" list. Use the "Reschedule" column to do just that, using your planner to write down the new time and date you will finish that task. If you have rescheduled something more than three times, evaluate why it is on your list at all and perhaps delegate it or remove it from the list altogether.

Protect your daily schedule. Deal with nonurgent interruptions by letting people know that you are working on a deadline and schedule a specific time to talk. Checking phone and email messages at particular times during the day, such as mid-morning and mid-afternoon, will help you stick to your agenda. Keep your work space organized by having a folder for each project or task. Once you've completed as much as possible on one task, put the folder away before starting on another project.

At the end of the day evaluate your achievements and be proud of what you've managed to get done. Create a new "To Do" list for the next day so that you can leave your work behind you and move into your personal time. Clear your desk, and leave work with the peace of mind of knowing that you've already taken control of tomorrow's time. We all feel swamped sometimes when we think about how much we need to get done in a day.

PLAN YOUR DAY THE EASY WAY

Exercise Thirteen
This exercise teaches a streamlined method of daily planning that is a quick and easy introduction to the concept.

1. *At the end of your day make a list of everything you hope to do tomorrow.*

2. *Choose the six most important tasks on your list and number them one to six.*

3. *When you begin your day, start with the number one task on your list and keep working on it until you have completed it or you've taken it as far as you possibly can.*

4. *Move to the second task and approach it the same way. Don't start the task until you've finished the second.*

5. *If you are called upon to deal with other tasks during the day, deal with them only if they are of greater importance than the task at hand. If a new item is not more important, simply add it to the bottom of your list of tasks to be prioritized when you revise the list at the end of the day.*

6. *When you have successfully completed the six items on your list or have done as much work on them as possible today, start compiling a fresh, prioritized list of tasks for tomorrow.*

7. *Even if you were not able to complete all six tasks that you had on your list by the end of the day, you have the satisfaction of knowing that you completed the most important ones.*

LONG-TERM PLANNING

If you don't know where you are headed, then any road will take you there. Exercises Nine to Eleven should already have helped you to identify some medium- and long-term goals. Now you are going to take a longer view.

One Hundred Things to Do in Your Lifetime
This is a great activity to do together as a family or group of friends. Children also love this activity, and it is great fun to

see how their list changes over time. Purchase some special notebooks or journals and give one to each person to write their list in and use over and over again as part of a yearly review.

The objective is to make a list of one hundred things that you would like to do in your lifetime. Think of as many as you can and add to your list when you think of new things, dating each entry. Don't restrict yourself by worrying about how much things cost or the likelihood of achieving something. Simply write down your dreams and wishes as they come to you. For example, your list might include: to travel around the world, to run a marathon, to write a book, or to climb Mount Everest. At the end of each year, take the time to review your list, to strike off what you have accomplished, and to add new items.

SET YOUR FIVE-YEAR GOAL

Exercise Fourteen
Making a five-year plan is no guarantee that you will achieve everything you wish to do in this period. But it does increase your chances of doing so. You can focus this exercise toward your personal life, or toward developing your career or business.

1. *Set aside some time, preferably a half day or even a weekend, to hold a five-year planning retreat. You can*

do this in your own home or go somewhere peaceful to create a greater sense of separation from your daily routine.

2. *Give yourself time to relax and then start to contemplate where you want to be in five years' time. If you've not yet done so, write your personal "Mission Statement." (see Exercise Ten). Answer the question "What is the purpose of my life?"*

3. *Ask yourself these questions too. What would be your ideal life five years from now? Where do you want to live? Do you want to live with someone or alone? How do you want to spend your days? Perhaps you want to be a parent and you see children in your life five years from now. Where would you like to see your business? Where do you see yourself on the career ladder? And so on.*

4. *Plan what proactive steps you need to take to make your dream a reality. Do you need to save a certain amount of money per year? Do you need to take a course? Do you need to meet new people? Set yourself yearly targets that will build toward your five-year goal.*

TIME MANAGEMENT AT WORK

Whatever type of work we do, we all have the same objective, which is to get as much work done as possible within the time allotted. One way to save time and be more efficient is to streamline the way we work and make better use of the tools available to us.

This chapter will help you manage your business contacts, show you how to declutter your office, teach you how to get the mounds of paper under control, and give you all the information you need to be able to take advantage of the latest time-saving technology. There are tips, too, on how to become the master of your telephone and e-mail so that you increase your productivity—and get home sooner.

In truth, people can generally make time for what they choose to do; it's not really the time but the will that is lacking.

Sir John Lubbock
(1834–1913)

PAPER MANAGEMENT

The advent of computer-based technology predicted the paperless office. However, you have only to look around most offices to know that this simply hasn't happened. A survey conducted in 2002 by the University of California found that offices around the world used 43 percent more paper than they did in 1999. It is estimated that 90 percent of all business information is captured on paper. Some experts contend that the average person spends 150 hours per year searching for lost or misplaced information from cluttered desks and files.

Managing the flow of paper into your office allows you to set up a system so you can process, store, and find important information. Get started by dealing with today's papers first; otherwise you will simply be creating another pile to deal with later on.

THE DAILY PAPER FLOW

- Deal with paper as it comes across your desk, then file it as soon as possible.
- When filing, place most recent papers on top in the folder so you can see the most recent correspondence every time you open the file.
- Designate an "In" tray for your daily incoming materials, and choose a routine time to sort and process these.

- Create a master list of all of your folders, which you can use as a quick reference guide. Your master list will also be helpful if a colleague needs to find certain paperwork when you are away from the office.

CLIMB THE PAPER MOUNTAIN

Exercise Fifteen
Contrary to popular practice, desktops are not effective places from which to manage the mountain of paperwork that is generated by most offices.

This exercise will help you organize and control your paper mountain.

1. *Decide what to keep and what to throw away by asking yourself the following questions: Does this information help my business? Will it improve my productivity somehow? Do I need to keep these papers now that the project/task is finished?*

2. *Create and use these folders to help you sort and keep track of all your papers:*
   Action – *Anything requiring your personal attention that you can't attend to while you are sorting out your papers. Make sure to add action items to your master*

"To Do" list so they won't be forgotten.
To Read – *Any magazine or newspaper articles you wish to read. Grab this folder when you are heading out of the office and you anticipate having some time to read, such as while commuting by train or waiting prior to an appointment.*
Pending – *Paperwork which you are awaiting a response to or further information.*
To File – *Stuff that needs to be filed away.*

3. *Depending on your type of work, you might also need other files, such as:*
   Delegate – *Any paperwork that someone else can take care of.*
   Ideas – *iI your work is of a creative nature, this is a great place to store your thoughts so that you can review and develop them.*
   Receipts – *Receipts for work-related expenses.*

DECLUTTER YOUR STUDY SPACE

Cluttered offices can be a source of stress, aggravation, and lost time. If your blood pressure increases as you survey the clutter, now is the time to do something about it. Assuming that you are not in a position to hire a professional organizer (everyone's dream!), ask a friend or colleague to help you remove temporarily as much from your office as possible, and pack things into boxes. If it is feasible, add a fresh coat of paint, wash or vacuum the floors, dust, and clean the windows. If not, do as much as you can yourself.

SORT YOUR CLUTTER INTO THESE GROUPS

- Things to have in your office—Keep only items that you need for your job, and avoid having more than one stapler, one notepad, and so on.
- Things to give away—If you haven't used something for two years or more, give it to your local charity or arrange to have them pick it up.
- Things to get fixed—Set aside time to get things fixed or to call the appropriate technician to do so.
- Anything else—If it doesn't fit in any of the above groups, take it home, or recycle it, or throw it away!

TIME-SAVING TECHNOLOGY

There are so many choices when it comes to technology that it is easy to be overwhelmed. When considering time-saving technology, ask yourself: Is the technology worth the investment of your time and money? Is it simple to use and easy to set up? How will it help you save time and/or become more productive? Is the product reliable and easy to get serviced?

COMPUTERS

It is very important to buy a computer suitable for the type of work you do. People who use their computer to design graphics have different requirements from those who use their machine as an electronic typewriter and filing system. Computer processing speed is measured in megahertz (mhz), and it makes economic sense to buy the fastest computer you can afford. Try to anticipate what you will need your computer to do two years from now, and buy a machine that can fulfil these requirements. How do you decide whether to buy a desktop or a laptop computer? If you know you need to use your computer in two or more locations, choose a laptop. If you travel a lot, a laptop will boost your productivity, allowing you to work at the airport or in your hotel room.

Time is the most valuable thing a man can spend.

Theophrastus
c.371–287 BCE

A high-speed internet connection, also known as broadband, is a real time saver when using the internet. If you don't have a high-speed connection, you can waste large chunks of your time downloading files or waiting for internet pages to open. The same goes for email, especially if you study in a technical or creative field, because email file attachments continue to get bigger. As the use of online video becomes more widespread for everything from music to the news, a broadband connection has become an essential workplace tool.

USB STICK

Mini or keychain drives are thumb-sized portable data-storage drives that provide you with immediate access to documents and files without the bother of bringing your laptop or CDs with you. Simple to use, mini drives offer the quick transfer of information simply by plugging them into the USB ports of computers. They are a great tool for people who often make presentations but don't want to carry around a laptop.

VIDEOCONFERENCING

Videoconferencing is a business tool that allows you to communicate with clients and coworkers around the world without leaving your office. The benefits include reductions in time spent flying, travelling, sitting in airport terminals, waiting in lines, and dealing with travel delays.

PRINTER

When buying a printer, the major time-saving consideration is speed. The speed of a printer is rated by pages per minute

—the higher the ppm the faster it prints. Printing color documents takes longer, which is an important factor if you typically print brochures, manuals, or graphics.

FAX

Although some people think that the fax machine is a technological dinosaur, it can still save you time in the office. Many computer programs allow you to send or receive faxes directly from your computer, but you will have to spend time scanning documents before you can send them, which can be very time consuming. Sometimes a regular, old-fashioned fax machine can get the job done in less time.

MULTIFUNCTION MACHINES

Investing in a multifunction machine that is a combination fax machine, copier, printer, and scanner can streamline a variety of processes that will save you time and money. But beware of using technology for technology's sake—only buy a machine with features that you need and know you will use, otherwise the purchase will be counterproductive.

MANAGING EMAIL

If you dread launching your email program because you receive so many emails, you are not alone. Studies show that

OFFICE DESIGN USING FENG SHUI

Feng shui (pronounced "fong shway") is based on the Eastern concept of chi, the energy life force. According to feng shui principles, if your office is organized correctly, the flow of chi will be smooth and harmonious, which will enhance your well-being and quality of life. An office with too much clutter traps chi" and can leave you feeling down and discouraged. Here are some guidelines for applying the principles of feng shui to your office.

- Clear clutter so that energy can circulate. Keep on your desktop only items that you need for the current task and things that really help you to be efficient.
- Arrange your office so that your desk faces the door and your back faces the wall. This is known as the "power position." According to feng shui you can watch as new business comes in the door and feel supported by the wall at your back.
- Fix or replace in a timely fashion anything that is broken, because things that don't work give off negative energy.
- Make your office an inviting environment. This will encourage you to get work done. Decorate it with items that bring you pleasure, such as inspirational artwork or photographs of loved ones.
- Make sure that you are physically comfortable. Get a good chair and make sure that your desk and computer are at the right height, your keyboard is in the correct position, and your phone is easily accessible.

If you are uncomfortable you will tire more easily and it will take you longer to get your work done.
- If your office is open plan, try to soften corners with plants to make the environment pleasant for everyone who works there.

we spend about two hours of each work day on emails—and this is likely to increase. Finding ways to manage email can help to reduce stress and increase your productivity.

Here are some frequently asked questions and answers about how to manage email and save time doing so.

How often should I check my email? This really depends on your situation. For most of us, checking email three times per day is sufficient—perhaps first thing in the morning, halfway through the day, and at the end of the day. Do not respond to email as it comes in. Many email programs have a message alert feature that will let you know when new mail has arrived. Unless you're required you to answer emails as they arrive or you are expecting an urgent email, turn off the message alert and stick to a regular schedule to check email.

What is the best way to handle mail in the in-box? Your

in-box should contain only email that you are waiting to read or that requires action. Set up your email program to sort mail automatically into predesignated folders. The aim is to deal with each email message once only, by responding, filing, forwarding, or deleting it.

How can I save time when sending and receiving email?
- Use the subject line to give the recipient an indication of what the email is about.
- Change the subject heading to reflect the content of the new message when replying.
- Be clear, concise, and to the point.
- Stick to one major subject per email, especially if you are requesting the recipient take action on a number of different items.
- Be clear about what action you are expecting from the recipient.
- Create a signature file (see your email program) that automatically includes your contact information at the end of each email.

How can email folders save time? If you receive more than ten emails per day, folders can be a great time-saving feature. You can separate important email from less important by setting up your email to recognize key words and direct the messages straight into project or client folders. These will make it easier for you to find crucial emails and less likely for them to get lost in the deluge.

When is it counterproductive to use email? Email is not the best option if you are dealing with an urgent matter and don't want to waste precious time. If you know the recipient is in their office or you can reach them on their cell phone, you have a better chance of resolving the issue quickly. If your response to an email would be long and involved, picking up the phone and having a conversation will save you time.

To choose time is to spend time.

Francis Bacon
(1561–1626)

TRACK YOUR PHONE TIME

Exercise Sixteen
Set up a phone log of your business calls so you can find out how much time you spend making and receiving phone calls. It will help down on unnecessary calls. You will need a large sheet of paper, a ruler, and a pen.

1. *Take the sheet of paper and draw eight columns using the ruler and the pen. Label them across the top from left to right: Date, Caller/Recipient's Name, Incoming/Outgoing Call, Voicemail, Duration, Reason for Call, Useful/Not useful.*

2. *Fill in the relevant columns as you use the phone for two weeks.*

3. *Add up the total amount of time you spent on the phone during each day, then the total for each week, and finally the total over the whole two-week period.*

4. *Now add up the amount of time spent on useful calls and then on calls that you didn't find useful. Review the reasons for the latter calls to see if a pattern emerges—it could be the same person calling, or perhaps you are trying to speak with someone but you keep missing each other. Consider taking action to eliminate calls that waste your time. For example, it might be easier to reach the person you keep missing by email.*

5. *Over the long term, use a notebook, your daily planner, or your contact-management software to keep a record of important telephone calls. jot down the key points of your conversations, as you might find this information useful in the future.*

PROJECT MANAGEMENT

Project managers strive to deliver on time and within budget a project with a distinct beginning and end, and

HOW TO CREATE A REALISTIC SCHEDULE

The project manager faces two major challenges: how to allocate enough time to meet the deadline, and how to recognize and avoid time-wasting obstacles. First, figure out how long each activity will take. Next, estimate how long it will take to complete the activity under ideal circumstances, and what resources are available, and when. Then, add in some extra time for unforeseen problems, delays, and contingencies, such as those below.

- Emergencies
- Staff absence and illness
- Subcontractor is late
- Equipment failure
- Late deliveries by suppliers
- Delays caused by the client
- Slow approval process
- Changes in requirements
- Public holidays

that uses specifically allocated resources, such as money, consumables, personnel, and time. Projects have a goal and an objective, and each project follows a logical sequence of events that makes use of the resources available to meet the project deadline. Ask the right questions. What is the project's objective? What are the start and finish dates? What resources do you need? What tasks do you need to accomplish? Who is responsible for which tasks?

When managing a project there are three constraints to balance: time, cost, and quality. We can view these as the sides of an equilateral triangle. And if one side grows, this generally affects the other sides.

As a project manager, you can lose credibility by underestimating the time required to complete a project. Understanding the scope of the project is the first step toward an accurate judgment of the time you will need. A detailed list of tasks that you need to accomplish should include the administration of the project, such as meetings, as well as the actual work. Be realistic and allow time for inevitable disruptions and delays.

Once the project is completed, ask yourself: was the project on time? If not, what external circumstances contributed to any missed deadlines? What circumstances over which you had control contributed to any missed deadlines? What will you do differently when estimating the time you require to finish the next project? Bear the answers in mind for the future.

TIME-WASTERS AND TIME-SAVERS

Looking back on your day with the feeling that you've wasted your time is frustrating. Time-wasters come in many forms and from all areas of our lives, both personal and professional.

This chapter will help you manage the mountains of information that you come across and will provide you with useful ways to deal with disruptions. Learning to manage meetings, to delegate, to say no, and to make use of your time when you have to wait, will turn your time-wasters into time-savers. Take the time to implement these ideas and you are on your way to becoming a good time manager.

INFORMATION OVERLOAD

There is no question that the technological advances which are part of our everyday lives have made many mundane tasks easier and faster to complete. However, the downside of technology is information overload. The massive amounts of information that come from a huge number

SAVE TIME WITH SPEED READING

One trick to help you keep up with important information is to increase the speed at which you read. First, determine your purpose before you start. Do you simply need to digest the main ideas? If so, skim-read. But if you need to assimilate more in-depth information, here are some tips.

- Read two or three (+) words at once and don't focus on every word.
- Avoid "saying" the words mentally as you read.
- Use a method to trace a path for your eyes to follow. For example, place your right hand on the right margin and move it slowly down the page, following the movement out of the corner of your eye.
- Don't reread phrases and sections of text. This will slow you down and will not necessarily help you understand the core ideas, as these are often elaborated as you continue to read.
- If you struggle with poor concentration when reading, start by focusing for five or ten minutes at a time.
- Look for key words and phrases that contain the main ideas and skim over less important words.
- Underline key phrases or ideas for quick reference later.
- If you have a lengthy document to read, survey the table of contents and read the summary or abstract so that you know how the information is laid out before you begin. This will also give you an idea of how difficult the material is and how much time you will need to cover it.

- Improve your vocabulary by looking up the meaning of any new words—especially jargon. Learning the relevant terminology will speed up your reading and comprehension in the future.
- Don't read when you are tired or feeling unmotivated—it's a complete waste of your time.

of sources, such as television, radio, emails, faxes, text messages, pagers, the internet, social media, newspapers, magazines, catalogues, and so on can be overwhelming

Combine the amount of information that comes your way on a daily basis with the limited number of hours in the day, and you have a recipe for time-related stress. In 1996 Reuters Business Information surveyed 1,300 managers about information overload. In the resulting report, 38 percent of them were stated as admitting they wasted "substantial" amounts of time collecting information. A significant number—3 per cent—said that their ability to make decisions was affected by what was termed "analysis paralysis," and 47 percent confessed that information collection distracted them from their main responsibilities.

The study also demonstrated that information overload is linked to stress: 43 percent of managers claimed to have suffered health problems caused by the stress of tracking, reading, and filing information. Also, 47 percent said that they took home work to keep up with the information they accumulated, which demonstrates that information overload had an adverse impact on their home life and leisure time.

How, then, is it best to manage information? Here are some different strategies.

When using internet search engines: have a clear idea of what you are looking for so that you can refine your search. Set a time limit when looking for information and accept that there is usually more available than you have time to access, so let some of it go.

Reduce the amount of books, video games, and other media you buy if you don't have time to read them all. When keeping magazines and newspapers, always throw one out for every new one you add. Use a reference librarian as an information gatherer. Many libraries have reference librarians who will search for information for you.

THE MANAGEMENT OF MEETINGS

Mention the "m" word and most people will tell you they have a love–hate relationship with meetings: "Can't work with them, can't work without them." Although meetings can be one of the most effective ways to discuss and exchange ideas and to make decisions, the general consensus is that many meetings are a waste of time—a reported 50 percent of meeting time is unproductive.

Professor Roger K. Mosvick's twenty-year analysis of who attends meetings and for how long found that, on average, executives spend 12 hours per week at meetings, middle managers spend 10.5 hours, and employees 8.5 hours. Other studies show that the average meeting lasts an hour and a half, that attendees are given an average of two hours' notice to attend, that 63 percent have no advance written agenda, and that 11 percent of the meeting time is spent on irrelevant issues. To plan and run a successful meeting requires a particular skill-set—thorough preparation, the ability to communicate clearly, and good time management.

TIME MANAGEMENT BEFORE MEETINGS

A well-written agenda for a meeting is clear and concise, with time allotted for each item. Prepare an agenda containing the following information: who is going to attend, the purpose of the meeting, where the meeting will be held, and when the meeting will start and finish. Organize your agenda with the most important items at the beginning and leave any new business until the end. Before you finalize it, give the attendees an opportunity to add discussion items. List the presenter next to each item and give ample time to prepare. Distribute copies of the agenda well in advance of the meeting. Also circulate in advance any material that will be discussed at the meeting to avoid wasting time reading them during the meeting itself.

TIME MANAGEMENT DURING MEETINGS

Show people that you value your time, and others', by starting meetings on time. Waiting for people, especially those who are chronically late, gives them the message that it's OK to run behind schedule. Once the meeting has begun, don't interrupt it to brief latecomers—that is simply wasting the time of the people who were prompt.

At the beginning of your meeting, remind participants how long it should last and take care to end at the stated time. Also, stick to the time limit you placed on the agenda items by letting people know when to wrap up, make a decision, and move on. Be diplomatic but firm. Invite people to continue a particular discussion in their own time after the meeting. Chances are you won't have any takers. Schedule your next meeting while everyone is still in the room to save yourself the aggravation of trying to accommodate everyone's schedules at a later date when they will be more booked up. Manage meetings effectively and you'll avoid Thomas Kayer's definition: "A meeting is an interaction where the unwilling, selected from the uninformed, led by the unsuitable, to discuss the unnecessary, are required to write a report about the unimportant."

MAKE YOUR MEETINGS MEANINGFUL

Exercise Seventeen

Unsure whether or not a face-to-face meeting is really necessary? Run through the following checklist to determine if you should go ahead:

- *You need a fast decision based on the input of the whole group or team.*
- *You need to resolve a group conflict.*
- *You want to brainstorm ideas.*
- *You want to share problems, weigh alternatives, and find solutions.*
- *The group wants to meet.*
- *To share success.*

Don't call a meeting ...
- *When you can use another form of communication instead.*
- *If you are not sure who should attend or key people cannot attend.*
- *If there is not enough time for you or the participants to prepare properly.*
- *When the cost in terms of time and money outweighs the benefits of what will be*

accomplished.
- *If you doubt that a meeting will achieve its objective.*
- *If you are avoiding making a decision.*
- *To reopen discussion about a decision that has already been made.*
- *If you simply wish to give out information.*
- *If there is a personal issue between you and a colleague or an employee.*
- *If people are angry and need time to cool down.*
- *If you or your group members are suffering from "meeting fatigue."*
- *If your group, executive, or team needs encouragement or a pick-me-up (plan a social get-together instead).*

DEALING WITH INTERRUPTIONS

Dealing with interruptions when trying to get your work done can make a short task drag on and on, upsetting your plans for the day and even the week. Sometimes we create our own interruptions by procrastinating or striving for perfection. At other times our personal life overlaps into our work time and friends call to chat or we get an email from the head of the school committee looking for a volunteer. Disruptions at work range from emails and phone calls, to people dropping by your office for legitimate work-related reasons or simply to socialize.

TRACK YOUR INTERRUPTIONS

Examine the interruptions and look for patterns. Are the same people doing the disrupting? Do the disruptions occur at a certain time of day? Do they happen in your office or when you are at a particular workstation? Are you being interrupted for the same reason?

STRATEGIES TO HANDLE OR MINIMIZE INTERRUPTIONS

Tell people not to interrupt you Use the technology at your disposal to let people know that you do not want to be disturbed. Record a voicemail message telling people that you are available to take and return calls between specific times only. You can do the same with your emails—create a return message that is sent automatically to each email received. If people know when you are available, they are less likely to interrupt you while you are busy.

Turn it off. Once you've notified people that you are not available, turn off the technology that allows them to contact you. Shut down your email, and switch off your pager and your cell phone.

Closed-door policy. An open-door office policy can be a big time-waster. Post a schedule listing your "open-door" time slots. Keeping your office door closed makes it less likely that you will be distracted by people walking past, and discourages people from entering your office to chat.

Conversation enders. How can you be diplomatic with people who monopolize your time? By being honest and telling them, "I honestly don't have time to talk right now." Then arrange a specific time with them, "I will be available at 4 p.m. for ten minutes. Is that a good time for you?"

ASSESS YOUR WORKLOAD

Exercise Eighteen
Use this quiz to find out if you have overcommitted yourself. Give the statements points according to the following scale: 0 = never 1 = sometimes 2 = mostly 3 = always. Then, add up the total to see which "zone" you are in.

- *I have difficulty getting out of bed to face the day because I have so much to do.*
- *I sometimes "freeze" with fear and anxiety about my workload.*
- *I usually work through my lunchtime.*
- *I feel angry and/or depressed because of my overloaded schedule.*
- *I have trouble delegating work or tasks to others.*
- *I rarely have a feeling of accomplishment.*
- *I find it impossible to say "no" to work.*
- *I volunteer to do things that I know I don't have time for.*

- *I lie awake worrying about how I'm going to get everything done.*
- *I feel guilty if I have time to myself because I think I should be doing something productive.*

Your score

Green Zone = 0 to 10	Yellow Zone = 11 to 20	Red Zone = 21 to 30
You seem to be managing your commitments skillfully, so keep on doing what you have been doing, because it is working well for you.	You are in the danger zone, so beware. Look for small ways to cut back on commitments and give yourself more time and space to breathe.	You are in commitment overload and you need to rethink your schedules and activities before there are serious consequences to your well-being.

HOW TO SAY "NO"

The ability to say "no" at the right time, with the appropriate tone of voice and body language, not only saves you time, but can preserve relationships. Time is a commodity, and often people ask us for our time because they don't have enough of their own.

Although an inability to say "no" can cause you to make too many commitments, it is more likely to be related to your personality than time-management skills. Most people dislike conflict and confrontation, and believe that saying "yes" avoids both—at least in the short term. Others are people-pleasers, who are motivated primarily by a desire to be liked by others, and they may also struggle with perfectionism.

You can say "no" without ever using the word "no," by using assertiveness skills. Being assertive means being able to communicate your opinions and feelings in an honest and clear fashion, in a way that respects the rights of others. For example, let's imagine that someone is asking you to be a committee member. Tell them you'd like to help but you cannot, and offer a brief, one-line explanation, such as "Right now my schedule won't allow me to take on anything new." (Although this is not always necessary, it might help to avoid a long conversation or further questions.) If the person persists, simply repeat that you'd like to help but you cannot, without any further explanation. Follow it with "It's been nice speaking with you," and move on.

What if a supervisor or manager at work asks you to take on more work? You can handle it diplomatically by asking them to decide which project they would like you to stop working on in order to fulfill their request. That puts them in position of making the decision and makes it clear what will and will not get done.

Never allow yourself to be pressured into giving a response on the spot. Be assertive and ask for time to think it over, especially if you know that you are having difficulty saying "no." Ask yourself, "If I say 'yes' to this what am I saying 'no' to?" before deciding.

HOW TO USE UNEXPECTED FREE TIME

Things to do in five minutes
- Clean out your handbag or briefcase.
- Listen to a guided visualization that takes you for a walk in the forest or on the beach.
- Start a load of laundry.
- Clean out a desk or kitchen drawer.
- Read an article from your "To Read" file.

Things to do in half an hour
- Take a nap.
- Go for a walk or a run.
- Call someone you care about.
- Fill out routine forms, such as license renewals and parking permits.
- Do the prep work for the next meal.
- Collect expense receipts and itemize them.
- Think about and jot down the agenda for your next meeting.
- Write a thank-you note to someone who was particularly helpful in the past week.
- Take a virtual tour on the internet of a country you would like to visit.
- Enter frequently called numbers into your cell, home, or office phone.

(continued on the next page)

(continued from the previous page)

• Go through your bookcase, remove any books that you haven't read or looked at for two years, and give them away to friends or donate them to a charity shop.

Things to do in half a day
• Review your goals.
• Visit a bookstore or library with comfortable seating, and read.
• Visit your favorite art gallery.
• Go for a beauty treatment.
• Invite a friend or colleague to meet you for coffee or tea.
• Declutter your filing cabinet by getting rid of old files.
• Clean up your computer by removing files that you no longer use.
• Organize your photos into albums.
• Bring a DVD with you when traveling and watch it on your laptop.
• Simply relax and do nothing!

Learning to say "no" takes practice, so start by saying "no" to small requests, and you will be surprised by how easy it becomes.

MAKING USE OF WAITING TIME

Many of us make the effort to call ahead when we have an imminent appointment, to determine whether or not the doctor or the hairdresser is running on time, or we always try to book our appointments for first thing in the morning or right after lunch to reduce the amount of waiting time. But no matter how carefully we plan, there will be times when waiting is simply unavoidable.

Although no one enjoys waiting in lines or getting delayed when traveling, you can make use of unexpected gaps of time by having a contingency plan to fill them. Use your waiting time—whether it's five minutes, half an hour, or half a day—to your advantage by doing small chores that are on your "To Do" list.

Another option is to make it your policy to enjoy unexpected free time and use it as a reward to do things that you like doing and wish you could do more often. For example, if you enjoy reading, make a habit of taking something to read with you when heading off to an appointment or using public transportation. This will also expand your vocabulary, or help you to keep abreast of developments in your profession or field of expertise, or let you escape mentally into a different world. If reading is not a favorite activity, try doing a crossword or a number puzzle, or make a gratitude list to remind yourself of good things in your life. Or you could simply take the opportunity to relax and unwind by closing your eyes and breathing slowly, deeply, and rhythmically.

TIME MANAGEMENT FOR EVERYONE

Everyone can make use of time-management skills to improve their quality of life and to work toward important goals. This chapter includes creative ideas to help teach both young and old about the value of time.

We start with children and how to instill in them the rudiments of time management. Next, we tackle students, because poor time management is the main culprit in academic failure, so learning how to create semester and exam schedules is vital. If you are a busy parent you will find plenty of time-saving tips as well as ideas to help you avoid overscheduling yourself and your kids, while those of you who are creative will discover some nontraditional approaches to time management. Finally, we look at the time-management challenges of retirement and discover ways to help you spend this time meaningfully.

TIME MANAGEMENT FOR CHILDREN

Anyone who has spent time around newborn babies knows that their needs and behavior—for example, sleeping in the day, and waking at night—do not fit easily with existing routines. But gradually babies adapt to their family's way of life.

Once children become toddlers, they are ready to learn about time. You can introduce them to the basics by showing them the difference between day and night, pointing out the time of day, and introducing the concepts of "before" and "after," using lunchtime as the divider. Teach little ones about the passage of time by talking about yesterday, tomorrow, the days of the week, the months, and the seasons.

TIME MANAGEMENT AND RESPONSIBILITIES

Although little children cannot read, they can follow pictures. To familiarize them with the idea of time management you can create a picture chart of their routine morning tasks, such as waking up on time, eating breakfast, and brushing their teeth. Buy some colorful stickers and let them place these beside each action they complete each day. At the end of the week offer a small treat as a reward for doing well.

Children between the ages of six and eleven are capable of learning how to manage their own time. You can begin by giving your child an alarm clock or clock radio on their sixth birthday and setting it for the time they need to get up in the morning on a school day. If your child is struggling to get everything done in the morning, reward them for each day they finish their checklist before heading off to school, and let them collect their reward at the end of the school week.

MAKE A COUNTDOWN CALENDAR FOR KIDS

Exercise Nineteen

Part of the fun in life is the anticipation we feel before important events.

Why not help yourself understand the concept of time by creating a countdown calendar to use in the run-up to a special day or event. Setting time limits, such as, "You have fifteen minutes more before you go to bed," will also help you to quantify the passage of time.

1. *Gather together a large, colorful sheet of paper, a pen, and a ruler. Decide how many days or weeks you wish the calendar to cover. (Avoid making the countdown last longer than three or four weeks—less on a calendar for a small child—as any longer might seem too far away, and they might lose interest.)*

2. *Take the pen and the sheet of paper and draw a grid containing one square to represent each day. Use the ruler to make sure that the lines are straight and the squares are roughly the same size. Alternatively, you could use a word-processing program to create and print out a grid from your computer.*

3. *Write the dates in the squares on the calendar, using another calendar for reference. The easiest way to avoid*

mistakes is to start at the end (the square in the bottom right-hand corner) by marking on the special day or event first, and work backward to the calendar's start date. When you have finished, check that you haven't missed out any days.

4. *Stick the chart on a wall somewhere where your child can reach it easily and will see it often, such as in the kitchen or in their bedroom. Get them to color in or cross off a square every day, thus counting down the days remaining until the big day or special event.*

PLAY TIME-RELATED GAMES

Have your parents guess how long it takes to do certain things. For example, how long do they think it takes to drive to Grandma's? Or how long does it take them to read their favorite story? This will help them to develop a sense of minutes and hours. You could also ask them to name as many things they can think of that last for set periods of time: say, for fifteen minutes, one hour, and so on.

MAKE TIME "PIZZAS"

Exercise Twenty
A time chart in the style of a pizza can show your child how they are spending their time, which will help to increase their time awareness.

SPENDING MY TIME

Using colored disks or coins will teach your child to spend their time wisely. You can draw, color, and cut out small circles. Different colored disks represent different time values, rather like casino chips (but don't worry, you won't be teaching your child to gamble!). For example, the red chip = 1 hour, the green chip = 30 minutes, and the blue chip = 15 minutes. Supply your child with the following amount of disks or coins: 12 red = 12 hours, 18 green = 9 hours, 12 blue = 3 hours. Your child pays you with colored disks before they "spend" their time on any activity they choose. This will help them understand that time is a valuable commodity and it will show them how they can make choices about how they use their time.

1. Using three large sheets of paper or three left-over pizza cartons and some brightly-colored pens, draw a large pizza on each sheet or carton. Get your child to help you to color them in and draw their favorite toppings on the pizzas.

2. Label the first pizza the "To-Do Pizza." Make a list of all the things that your child has to do in a typical day. Have them prioritize the most important tasks to the least important, and get them to estimate how long each item will take to do. Divide the pizza into time slices using the prioritized list and estimates.

3. *Name the second pizza the "Hour-by-Hour Pizza." This will show how your child actually spends each hour of a typical day. Divide the pizza into twenty-four "slices" and number them for each hour. Starting with the time at which your child gets up, label each segment according to the main activity in that hour—for example, breakfast, schoolwork, playtime, sleep, and so on. Divide up the day until you return to the start.*

4. *Call the third pizza the "Activities Pizza" and divide it into twelve two-hour time slices. With your child count up how many hours they spend on different activities. Point out how it all adds up to twenty-four hours.*

5. *Compare the pizzas to see how your child's priorities and estimates compare with how they really spend their time.*

Another good game will help your child to understand the difference between seconds and minutes. You will need an alarm clock or a kitchen timer and a watch or clock with hour and second hands. Ask your child to watch the clock as you point out when the second hand moves from zero to five seconds, then from zero to thirty seconds, and finally from zero to sixty seconds. Discuss which felt longest to them. Explain that sixty seconds means the same thing as one minute.

Next, set the alarm or timer for two minutes and ask your child to dance to some favorite music. When the two minutes are up, set the alarm or timer for another two minutes and this time get the child to sit still and stay quiet until the timer goes off. Then, ask them which seemed to them to last longer: the time spent dancing or the time spent sitting still? Why?

Finally, have them make some guesses about how long ordinary things take, such as setting the table, boiling the kettle, putting away toys, and tying their shoelaces. Let them check the accuracy of their guesses using the watch or the timer.

LEARNING TO RESPECT TIME

Encourage yourself from an early age to be on time. This will teach you to respect your own time and everyone else's. Look at how everyone spends their time by filling in a pie chart to represent an average school day. Ask them to point out any times when they run into time conflicts. Then, take a typical activity, such as getting ready for soccer practice. Break it down into five-minute increments so that you learn the steps involved in getting ready and how long it actually takes to get all these things done.

Discuss the fact that being on time is a sign of respect for the coach and their teammates. If you're habitually late, you need to deal with the natural consequences. This teaches everyone the cause-and-effect relationship between the choices they make and the consequences.

Continually nagging children to hurry up is distressing for everyone. Clearly state your expectations:

We always have time enough if we will but use it properly.

Johann Wolfgang von Goethe
(1749–1832)

TIME MANAGEMENT FOR STUDENTS

Poor time management is the main culprit behind academic failure. Whether you are in high school or beyond, as the workload increases, you can't do well in school if you are always pushed for time.

Let's start with the big picture. What are your goals related to school? What do you want to accomplish? How will you benefit by completing this stage in your academic career? How do you imagine that your life will be improved? How will you feel about yourself, having completed this degree or program? Staying connected to your goals will motivate you to keep your time-based priorities in the proper order: designate time for school first, and fit the rest of your life around it.

HOW MUCH TIME DO YOU SPEND?

It's unlikely that you will be able to improve how you manage your study time unless you get an idea of where all your time goes. Start by estimating how much time you spend on the following in any given week:

- Sleeping and eating
- On personal hygiene
- On chores and personal errands
- Playing sports or exercising
- Watching TV or using the computer
- Socializing with friends
- Spending time with family
- In class
- Studying and reading commuting
- Working

The next step is to keep track of the actual amount of time you spent on each item. Is there a difference between your estimate and the actual? This will give you an idea of the adjustments you need to make—which activities you need to reduce and where you need to invest more time in order to meet your school-related goals.

ARE YOU TIME-WISE?

Respond to the following statements either "Yes" or "No" to determine your current time-management situation.

- I write things down.
- I use a daily "To Do" list.
- I plan for the coming week.
- I know what is due next month.
- I complete assignments on time.
- I schedule time to study for exams.
- I know how long each assignment will take.
- I use a time-management planner.
- I treat my schoolwork like a job.
- I put schoolwork before other activities and leisure time.

The more "Yes" responses you have, the better your time-management skills are.

SCHOOL PLANNERS

Many schools and institutions publish a combination day planner and student handbook, which includes important dates such as examinations, course dates, fee-payment deadlines, and so on. School planners are based on the school year and they run typically from August to the following July. Most use a week-at-a-glance layout over two pages, along with the entire month on one page at the beginning of each month.

MAKE GOOD USE OF YOUR STUDY TIME

Before you begin an assignment, make a rough assessment of how long it will take to complete. Write a list of the steps required to get it done. Include research time, consulting with your professor, and so on. Estimate how long each step will take and add up the total—now double it!

Assess when you best like to study. Are you an "owl" or a "lark"? If you like to get up early, enjoy attending early morning classes, and do your best work before 3 p.m., chances are you are a "lark." But if you feel best in the later part of the day and like to do school work in the evening and into the night, you are an "owl." If you are an "owl" you may have a more difficult time because school schedules favor "larks." Knowing when you work best will help you make good use of your time: study when your attention-span is at its peak and do routine tasks at other times. Procrastination is a common problem for students in higher education, with approximately one third of students stating that it interferes with their academic achievement. If you have a procrastination problem, tackle it now—Exercise Four will show you how.

CREATE A SEMESTER SCHEDULE

Exercise Twenty-One

This exercise shows you how to compile a semester schedule, which will give you a bird's-eye view of what you need to do to fulfill your course requirements.

1. *Using a computer, print out a monthly calendar—one for each month in the semester. Or, if you prefer, buy a large, wipe-clean wall calendar from the school bookstore or an office supply store. Better still, have both: a monthly calendar to keep with your agenda and a large calendar posted near your desk to use as a visual reminder to help you stay on track.*

2. *Take the school handbook and list important institutional dates, such as registration dates, assignment deadlines, exam schedules, and payment due dates.*

3. *Gather together all your course outlines and lists of assignments. Taking one course at a time, write on your calendar(s) the dates of exams, presentations, and when essays and so on are due. Also, mark how much each exam and piece of work contributes toward the*

121

final grade (for example, an essay might be worth 10 percent). This will help you to plan how much time to allocate for each item.

4. *Include any important personal one-off dates, such as birthdays, and special family and social events, so that you can plan your school work around them.*

5. *Make a note of any weeks in which you have more than one exam or assignment due, and do as much in advance as you can to avoid last-minute cramming and having to rush your assignments.*

If you find it easy to get down to studying, a good approach is to start your sessions with your most difficult, least-liked subjects. You will concentrate better and retain more information when you are fresh, and you will also motivate yourself by getting the hardest tasks out of the way.

Study where the distractions are fewest. If being at home makes it too tempting to turn on the TV or to head for the kitchen, go to the school library instead. But make sure that you take a five-minute break every half hour, especially when studying for exams. Studying for longer than half-hour blocks of time makes you increasingly ineffective. Avoid the temptation to take longer breaks by establishing a routine—for example, make a cup of tea, or take a short walk through the library. Try to review your class notes on a daily basis. This will help to consolidate the material in your memory and will reduce the amount of time you will need to revise for exams.

BALANCING SCHOOL AND YOUR SOCIAL LIFE

Part of the school experience is social life. In order to do well in school it is important to have a social life but, as in all things, within reason. Including your fun time in your planner will help you balance friends and school. Plan your social life around your school life and not vice versa. Designating every Friday night as a going-out night gives you something to look forward to and breaks up the week. Avoid the tendency to join too many clubs and activities—especially at the beginning of the school year.

MAKE A WEEKLY SCHEDULE

Exercise Twenty-Two
Sunday evenings are a great time to plan for the coming week. This exercise will show you how to schedule the week ahead.

1. *Use your planner, or print out a weekly template from your computer on which you can enter class times once for the whole semester. Fill in regular features, such*

as lectures and tutorials, and add the deadlines for assignments and tests. Include your work hours for the week along with any other non-study commitments.

2. *Map out your study time for the week ahead, bearing in mind the level of difficulty you have with each individual course. Some courses will require you to put in more effort, others will take less preparation and study time. Take into account the amount of reading you need to do and allow time for note taking.*

3. *Schedule the most difficult or least interesting tasks for times when you are at your peak mentally.*

4. *Don't overfill your schedule, and be realistic about how much you can accomplish, especially after a full day of classes and working part-time. Leave time for relaxing, socializing, and going out.*

5. *Don't be afraid to revise your schedule according to your needs. Learning to juggle study with work is a valuable part of your education.*

6. *Use your weekly schedule to create your daily "To Do" list.*

BALANCING SCHOOL AND WORK

If while you are attending school you are also working, you will undoubtedly be time-pressured. Don't work for more than twenty hours per week as this will not only jeopardize your chances of success, but also increase your chances of dropping out. Look for work close to your home or to the campus to reduce traveling time. Many colleges and universities hire students and also offer programs where you can alternate a school semester with a work semester. Or take one less course per term—this will allow you to work enough hours to meet your financial commitments. You are also likely to get better grades if you have fewer courses to work on.

CREATE A STUDY SCHEDULE FOR EXAMS

Exercise Twenty-Three
When your exams come around—and they always arrive quicker than you think—you need to know how much study time you'll need to get the grades you deserve. This exercise will help you schedule your time well in the run-up.

> 1. *To determine how much time to spend on studying a specific course, make sure that you know its percentage*

THE 2:1 TIME-RATIO RULE OF THUMB

The higher the level of education, the greater investment of time required. As a general rule, at college and university level you should spend two hours studying for every hour you are in the classroom. If you spend twelve hours per week in class you should schedule twenty-four hours of preparation and study. That's thirty-six hours of your week dedicated to school.

You will probably need to make adjustments as you learn what works best and how to handle obstacles. Keep in mind your goal of graduating to motivate you when you have to juggle endless classes, assignments, and exams. Once you put some time-management strategies into place, redo the "Are You Time-Wise?" quiz to see how you have improved.

contribution toward your overall grade. For example, if one exam is worth 20 percent and another is worth 80 percent, you should allocate more time to study for the latter.

2. *Approximately four weeks before the exams, prepare your study schedule. Make a list of exams and their dates for each course, and work out how much time to spend on each. Then, total up the total amount of hours you'll need to study.*

3. *Using the exam dates, work backward, filling in two-hour blocks of study time. Studying in two-hour time blocks with short breaks in between prevents fatigue and time wasting.*

4. *Distribute your study time over the four weeks prior to your exam, because spacing helps you to retain more information than cramming in one long study session.*

5. *Don't forget to schedule enough sleeping time during your pre-exam period. Deep, restorative sleep helps to consolidate information into your long-term memory. Staying up all night to study is not a productive use of your time, and writing exam papers when you are exhausted is not a great strategy for success.*

TIME MANAGEMENT FOR FAMILIES

Being a parent is the ultimate time-management juggling act. A parent's life has three simultaneous cycles—the school cycle, the work cycle, and the family cycle, each with competing and sometimes conflicting demands.

SPENDING MORE TIME WITH YOUR FAMILY

Time spent with parents is often the first thing to suffer when we are experiencing a time crunch. Above all else, our children want—and need—our time. Studies around the world reflect the comments of Barbara Moses, the expert in career management, "The time famine in North American society does not just affect working adults. Children are starved, too—starved of meaningful time spent with their parents."

Children want presence, not presents. Toys and gifts will often be forgotten, but many of our best memories are of time spent together going to a baseball game, going on an outing, or taking a walk in the park. Review the past month and take an honest look at how much time you spend with your children. Add up the total number of hours and divide this by the number of days to give yourself the average time spent on a daily basis. Now that you've looked at the quantity, take a look at the quality of the time you've spent with your family. For example, if you are home with your children and they spend most of their time in another room watching TV, it could be said that this isn't a good use of your time together. A simple yet effective way to resolve this would be to remove televisions from your bedrooms, create one TV room in your home, and make watching television a family activity.

There are many other ways to increase the quantity and quality of time you spend with your family. You could designate one night per week as your family fun night (but then you must stick to this and not let work or other commitments impinge, otherwise you will disappoint the family immensely.) Or, have a pajama day where everyone in the family spends the day in their nightclothes while reading, playing games, or just loafing around.

Exercising together by going for a walk, a run, playing soccer, or doing any kind of sport is another great way to have fun and spend time with your family—and it'll keep you healthy too. You can also involve your children more in the running of the household by getting them to help you with chores, such as preparing meals. Eat meals together whenever possible—studies have shown that the frequency of family dinners is the single most accurate predictor of children's academic achievement and psychological well-being.

SEPARATION AND DIVORCE

When parents live apart there are unique time-management challenges because children need to spend time with each parent in his or her home. If parental communication is good, you can create a timetable together on the phone at the beginning of each month. Alternatively, sending a timetable with the child as they visit the other parent will give you both an opportunity to stay current and be reminded of upcoming events. Some families use online interactive calendars that both parents can access to flag any changes for the other parent to see.

THE VALUE OF UNSCHEDULED TIME

These days there is pressure to get our children involved in an ever-increasing amount of extra-curricular activities, such as sports, dance, and music. This pressure has spawned the "hyper parent" who overschedules their children to the point of burnout. Instead, we need to rediscover the value of unscheduled time, and include time for kids to relax, daydream, and play outdoors.

CREATE A "COMMAND CENTER"

Exercise Twenty-Four
Every family needs a "command center" and the calendar is a great tool.

This exercise will show you how to set up and run your command center.

1. *Designate an area of your kitchen to be your communication center. Here you will keep your master calendar (see step 2), a notebook and pen for recording telephone messages, a list of emergency phone numbers (see box, opposite), and a folder for each of your*

SAVING TIME IN AN EMERGENCY —AT HOME

Being prepared in the event of an emergency will save you precious time when time is at a premium. It is easy to become disoriented when coping with stressful situations, so it is important to keep a list of phone numbers and addresses at hand in a pre-arranged place. Teach your children how to make an emergency phone call. Make sure you include your own address on your list in case a friend or relative is visiting and they have to make an emergency phone call on your behalf. Here are the basic phone numbers to include:

• Police, fire, and ambulance (these are usually on the same number) • Mom's work number • Mom's cell phone • Dad's work number • Dad's cell phone • Grandparents' numbers • Other family numbers • Local hospitals • Neighbors' numbers • Close friends' numbers

children to hold information about school, and any activities they do.

2. Print out or purchase a calendar (showing one month per page) and insert it into a ring binder. This is your master calendar for the year, on which you can write any important dates up to a year in advance.

3. *Print out or purchase a large wall calendar that shows both the current month and the forthcoming month, and hang it on the wall in your communication center, so that all family members can read it. Then, using your master calendar, transfer all the information for the current and coming months onto the wall calendar. (Enlist your children's help—it's a job that many school-aged children will enjoy.)*

4. *Along with everyone's activities and commitments, include dates when either parent will be away, and any temporary changes that will affect regular arrangements.*

5. *Each evening check out the next day's activities and encourage your children to consult the calendar by marking surprise treats such as taking them to a movie or going out for Sunday brunch.*

A good way to avoid overscheduling is to limit your children to one activity per category at any one time. For example, one sport per season usually entails two practices and a game per week—enough for most children. Set aside time each week for unplanned activities with your children. Give them three options, which include opportunities to talk and interact, and let them choose (but ban electronic toys). You could also ask teachers to institute a "no-homework" night once a week or one weekend per month. You are bound to get the support of your children on this one!

WORKING FROM HOME

It takes self-discipline to work effectively at home. It takes self-discipline with yourself to be at your desk by a specific time each day, and set yourself certain office hours, which you stick to. It is also helpful to make time visible by keeping a large ticking clock in front of your desk in your line of sight. However, make sure that you take regular breaks—this is just as important at home as it is in the workplace. Step away from your desk at scheduled intervals for a short time. Overworking is not productive and can turn into workaholism, which can damage your health and well-being, your family relationships, and even your business.

FAMILY TIME-MANAGEMENT TIPS

- Getting everyone out of the door in the morning can be one of the most stressful times for a family. Prepare as much as possible the night before—pack lunches and organize clothes and backpacks.
- Teach your children to make their own breakfast during the school week. Place the non-perishable breakfast items along with the utensils on the table the night before.

(continued on the next page)

(continued from the previous page)

- Make sure that the kids know how to put dishes in the dishwasher and to clear the table when they are finished.
- Supply each child with a wicker or plastic basket to keep their hats, gloves, and scarves in. Store the baskets in the hall.
- Teach your children how to sort their laundry by using color-coded laundry baskets. Use a white basket for whites, navy for dark colors, and red for other colors. This way, laundry has to be sorted only once.
- Establish and maintain (as far as possible) household routines for meals, homework, and chores. Do cleaning on one day and food shopping on another. Ask your partner to spend time with the children while you go food shopping, and vice versa—that way you each share the fun and the chores.
- Lower your standards for the unimportant—no one really cares if the floor gets vacuumed every second week instead of every week. Do home baking if it is a family activity, otherwise store-bought items are just fine. Resist the urge to do everything yourself: call on the troops when you need to.
- Set up an "in" and an "out" basket for each child in which they can dump their school-related papers to be filled out, signed, and returned to school.
- Pay bills online using the internet. This is a tremendous timesaver and you can do it in the comfort of your home at a time that is convenient for you.
- Have a short family meeting every weekend at a time convenient for everyone to preview the coming week.

There are no end of distractions to face when you are working at home. They range from the family to the dog, the refrigerator and the TV. Then there's the ever-present reminder of all the housework that you need to do. Here are four of the most common distractions that people come up against when working from home, with tips on how to deal with them:

The kitchen. Having free access to the refrigerator is just too tempting a distraction for some of us. Try to stick to a regular coffee break and lunch routine. Keep a pitcher of water and a glass at your desk to avoid getting up from your desk unnecessarily. Stock a small refrigerator in your office with health-boosting fruit and salad vegetables to snack on.

Television. If you have a favorite show that is on in the middle of your working day, record it, and watch it in the evening or on the weekend. However, if you simply must see the program, schedule it into your day and do some exercise or stretches while watching it. This will help you to avoid feeling guilty for not working and allow you to do something good for yourself at the same time.

Family and friends. Somehow family and friends make the assumption that if you are at home, you can't really be working. If people drop in often and disrupt your working day, be honest, and tell them in a friendly but firm way that you don't have time to socialize now. Instead, arrange to see them later for dinner or coffee. Put a sign saying "Do Not Disturb" on your office door to discourage unnecessary interruptions. (Place it on your front door if family and friends continue to intrude on your work time.)

Caller ID is a great tool for screening your phone calls. You can return personal calls during your lunch time or at the end of the day, much as you would if you worked away from home. Or you could ask other family members at home to screen personal calls while you are working. Ask them to tell callers that you are busy and cannot come to the phone and to take messages so that you can call them back later.

Household chores. It is amazing how interesting doing the laundry can be when you are facing a big assignment and don't feel like working! One way to deal with household chores when you are working from home is to schedule in, say, half an hour of cleaning or washing at the time of day when your energy for work-related tasks is low. Or make a schedule whereby you clean one room per day. Doing some housework can be invigorating, and if you keep to a set schedule for the week, you will get everything done without being tempted to do too much at once.

Separate work and home by shutting your office door at the end of your working day. If you don't have a separate office, shut down your computer and put away your work materials. Although many people imagine that they will have more time to spend with their families by working at home, the reality is that most home workers usually end up putting in longer hours than their counterparts who go to work in offices.

Those who make the worst use of their time are the first to complain of its shortness.

Jean de la Bruyère
(1645-96)

TIME MANAGEMENT FOR CREATIVE PEOPLE

Our brains are divided into left and right hemispheres, with each hemisphere specializing in a thinking style. The capabilities of the left brain include analytical thinking, reading, writing, and mathematical ability. The right brain focuses on non-verbal skills—visual, perceptual, spatial, and intuitive abilities. The left brain processes pieces of information in a sequence while the right brain synthesizes information as a whole.

Creative people are considered to be "right brainers" and they often balk at the analytical approach taken by time-management systems. Here are some commonly perceived myths about creativity and time management, and some suggestions for how to resolve them.

"Trying to control my time destroys my creativity and makes me feel anxious."

This is a classic misconception because if you allocate time in which to do creative work, you will have peace of mind and feel free to focus 100 percent on your creativity. It makes sense to reserve chunks of time so that you can concentrate on what you love to do. Try one day on and one day off or even one week on and one week off. While away from your creative work, keep a spiral notebook at hand and jot down your ideas. For shorter blocks of time, remove your watch or clock, and set a timer to go off in another room when your time is up. That way you won't be distracted by clock-watching.

"I wait until I feel inspired before I move into my 'creative space.'"

This is a luxury that few can afford—most successful artists, musicians, and writers "show up" and get down to work regardless of their mood. Try establishing a routine and use it to make your transition into work mode. For example, you might make a cup of tea, put on your favorite sweatshirt, and then gather up your work materials. Find a routine that works and use it every time you want to move into your creative space.

"As a creative person I don't need to set goals—I prefer to just go with the flow and see what happens."

Unless you are independently wealthy, you do need to have goals in order to make a living. If you make your living doing creative work, perhaps as a writer, a graphic artist, a painter, or a musician, keep yourself motivated to complete goals by staying connected to your vision. Get back in touch with your passion and you'll automatically get into the flow.

"I do my best creative work when I am up against a set deadline."

In fact, research shows the opposite—that the more time pressure creative people experience, the less creative they feel. This is intensified when people are distracted by trivial tasks, sudden changes in plans, or if they do not feel that the work they are doing is important. Creativity can flourish under time pressure, but only if there is a shared sense of purpose and if all those involved can focus their energy without interruptions. If you are part of a team, ask for clarification when you are unsure as to why you are attempting to accomplish something. A clear purpose will help you to refocus. Protect your creative time from distractions and interruptions and, if possible, find a quiet place away from the workplace where you can complete your project in peace.

"Part of being creative is working alone, without having to be accountable for my time to anyone."

We all need to be accountable to someone to grow and develop. Try making a commitment to a colleague to do a certain task by a certain time. Or agree with peers, for example in your art class, that you will accomplish a certain piece of work and bring it along to the next meeting.

TAKE ADVANTAGE OF YOUR CREATIVE TIME

Exercise Twenty-Five

If you struggle with finding time to pursue your creative activities, use this exercise to help you take advantage of each precious moment by creating your own portable, artistic space.

1. *Some creative pursuits, such as writing, painting, and drawing, are highly portable. The key to taking full advantage of creative time is to have your kit prepared and ready to use as soon as inspiration strikes.*

2. *If you enjoy writing, you might like to include the following in your kit: a notebook; a list of questions to use as writing prompts; a small collection of your favorite quotes written on cue cards; your favorite writing tools (a ball point pen, a pencil, a fountain pen, a felt-tip, and so on). Purchase an inexpensive three-ring binder and divide it into sections using clear plastic dividers with pockets to store your quotes, your notebook, and so on. Another portable option might be to stock your writing supplies in a small case or tote bag that you can easily slip into a briefcase if you are heading to the office, or that can be carried on its own.*

MAKE A WEEKLY "TO DO" FLOW CHART

Traditional "To Do" lists not for you? Then, why not use a flow chart to make a bright, colorful list instead? You will need a large sheet of paper and a variety of colored markers.

To create a weekly "To Do" flow chart, start in the middle of the page and draw seven large arrows, each in a different color, facing outward in a circle. Label each one with the name of a day of the week. Think about what you want to do this week and on which day. Then, write out each day's tasks next to its arrow in the color you chose to represent that day. Or if you prefer, draw little pictures of the tasks instead of writing them out. Repeat this process until you've filled the week to your satisfaction. Update your flow chart and add new items or ideas as the week progresses.

3. *If you like to paint or draw you must plan your portable art kit carefully so that you are not carrying your entire studio with you. Consider purchasing a molded plastic briefcase type of tote bag to hold your papers, pads, pens, pencils, pastels, paints, and brushes. Or you could get yourself an organizer on wheels (the type used for carrying a computer) which would be a great choice to hold your supplies.*

It's not enough to be busy—so are the ants.

Henry David Thoreau
(1817–62)

MAP YOUR RETIREMENT

Exercise Twenty-Six

Most of us are so busy working that we've not given much thought to what will happen when we retire. Mapping out how you want to experience the future will help you prepare for and make the transition smoothly.

1. *Get yourself a journal in which to record your ideas for a perfect future. Use it to note down your thoughts, to explore your feelings, and to ask yourself questions about the next several years.*

2. *Title a page: "Things I've always wanted to do but never had time to do" and list as many activities as you can think of. (Or, if you prefer, draw pictures of the activities instead of writing them.) Next to each item write why you would like to do it and, if possible, set a target date by which you would like to accomplish it.*

3. *Label a second page in your journal: "I am happiest when ..." and list all the things that you really enjoy doing. Write down what it is about these things that make you happy.*

THE FUTURE AND SELF-ACTUALIZATION

According to the psychologist Abraham Maslow (1908–70), self-actualization is the process of reaching one's full potential—and what better time to pursue personal growth than in retirement? People who are self-actualized have certain characteristics, the main ones of which are listed below. Which ones apply to you?

- I am spontaneous in thought and action.
- I accept myself and others.
- I feel connected to, and a kinship with, others.
- I value my individuality.
- I am self-sufficient.
- I enjoy spending some time alone.
- I have a mission and a purpose in life.
- I do not fear the unknown.
- I am able to understand the lesson in most life situations.
- I feel alive and enjoy life.
- I like to do things that help and benefit others.
- I like to learn new things.

The more descriptions that apply to you, the more self-actualized you are. Review the activity groups above for how to become more well-rounded.

4. *Head a third page: "Things I never want to do again"
and make a list of any activities that you want to banish
from your vision of adulthood.*

5. *Using all the notes and lists you made above as
reference, write a definitive description of your
retirement, covering where you would like to live and
how you would like to spend your time.*

6. *Review and update your description regularly as you get
closer to your retirement.*

VISUALIZE A POSITIVE RETIREMENT

Exercise Twenty-Seven
Visualization is a form of meditation that will help make
a positive retirement a self-fulfilling prophecy. When you
visualize, you are creating a mental movie that you can tap
into anytime, anywhere.

1. *Take the journal you used in Exercise Twenty-Six
and find yourself a comfortable, quiet place in which
to sit—perhaps a peaceful room at home, outside in a
favorite spot in your garden, or in the local park.*

2. *Read through your journal and concentrate particularly
on the summary you wrote describing your perfect
retirement. Read through this part several times.*

3. *Close your eyes, breathe in deeply, and exhale slowly. Let any tension drain away from your body and try to relax totally. Breathe rhythmically in this way for a few minutes.*

4. *Think about your journal description of your perfect retirement and bring it to life by picturing yourself starring in your very own "movie." Explore different scenarios. Imagine where you live, your family life, your friends, your physical and intellectual activities, and how you live your life purpose. Engage all of your senses: see the glorious colors of the flowers; hear your grandchildren's voices; feel the soft fur of your pet cat; smell the aroma of the bread you are baking; taste the delicious food at the restaurant; and so on.*

5. *Repeat the visualization as often as you wish. Conjuring up a mental picture of your ideal retirement will help you make it real.*

CONCLUSION

Now that you've read through the book I hope that you have a sense of how your life will be different once you've taken back control of your time. What would it feel like to know that you have time to do the things that are important to you? That you are working toward your goals? That you have time to spend with family and friends? Imagine a life with less stress and fear, and more personal satisfaction and joy. That's what getting a handle on managing your time can do for you.

I would like to think that you will use this book as a reference to manage your time, yourself, and your life. Choose a time-management method that works, is simple to use, and fits easily into your life. Studies show that successful people go the extra mile and keep track by writing things down, especially their goals. Use the exercises in this book to do the same.

You now have at your disposal all the tools and techniques you need, so why not go one step farther and make a commitment to becoming the best time manager possible? Try to make time management a natural part of your everyday life to the point where you would no sooner go through your day without managing your time than you would without brushing your teeth. Invite a friend or colleague to be your time mentor to keep you motivated and accountable.

Of course, bear in mind that from time to time we all feel overwhelmed and discouraged. When this happens your life will get out of balance and you will find that demands on your time are impossible to meet. Sometimes it will simply be a case of having lapsed into managing your time poorly. For example, perhaps you managed your time well as a student but now you are finding it difficult as a young parent or as a business person—or both! When you find that you are struggling, reread the sections of this book that apply to your particular stage of life. Then, take a deep breath, make some tough decisions about what you can and cannot do, and start again. Don't be discouraged—even very successful people experience difficulties at some point in their lives. What makes the difference is having the resilience to work through your difficulties, and finding the motivation to start again. After all, if you have done it once, you can do it again.

Be fiercely protective of your time and defend your right to spend it in the way that is most beneficial to you and your family. Remember that your personal legacy will be determined by how you spend your time today—and tomorrow, and the next day. Regardless of your age, always live your life with a sense of urgency, in the knowledge that time is passing. Resolve to be aware and mindful of the present, each and every day. Ultimately, it's your time and your life. You get to choose how you spend it. Start managing your time today so that you can, quite literally, have the time of your life.

GLOSSARY

ABDOMINAL BREATHING: A method of breathing using your diaphragm to help calm yourself.

ANALYSIS PARALYSIS: A term coined by a 1996 Reuters Business Study to identify the overwhelming feeling people get when trying to sort through the information overload they handle in a given day, especially online.

CHRONOS: Literal clock time measured by hours, minutes, and seconds.

COMMAND CENTER: The place in your house where you keep all your schedules and resources for time management

80/20 RULE: Also known as the Pareto Principle, it's the idea that 20 percent of time and efforts creates 80 percent of the results or vice versa.

HOROLOGY: The study of time management.

HURRY SICKNESS: A term coined by doctors Meyer Friedman and Ray Rosenman in the 1950s, while studying personality types. Its symptoms are lack of time, too much to do in too little time, or being upset by any kind of delay.

KYROS: Subjective time "feel."

PERFECTIONIST: A person who struggles with self-imposed unrealistic standards and expectations

PROCRASTINATION: Putting off a job until the last minute possible, from the Latin *pro cras*, meaning "for tomorrow."

PRODUCTIVITY PYRAMID: A way to organize your priorities with your overall principles as the base, your long-term goals in the next layer, your intermediate goals above that, and your daily goals at the top. Also known as the Pyramid Principle.

PRIORITY PRINCIPLE: A four-category method of organization to determine what's the most important and what's a lower priority.

PROJECT MANAGEMENT: In the business world, project management ensures the details of a project, from schedule to finer points.

QUALITY TIME: Spending your free time in a meaningful manner.

SMART: An acronym to help you plan your goals—specific, measurable, attainable, realistic, time-lined.

TIME BUDGET: Your activities for a week compared to how many actual hours are available total.

TIME PIZZAS: Time charts in the shape of pizzas to help you or a younger child to identify everything that needs to be done day by day or hour by hour.

2:1 TIME-RATIO RULE OF THUMB: Two hours of studying for every hour in the classroom.

VISUALIZATION: A form of meditation in which you create a picture of the role or relaxation you want to achieve.

WORKAHOLIC: Someone who feels great anxiety when idle and who has bad personal relationships.

FOR MORE INFORMATION

Big Future, The College Board
250 Vesey Street
New York, NY 10281
212-713-8000
https://bigfuture.collegeboard.org
This is a website for college-planning teens, maintained by the
   College Board.

Brooklyn Public Library
10 Grand Army Plaza
Brooklyn, NY 11238
718-230-2100
http://www.bklynlibrary.org/explore-topic/teens/get-things-
   done-time-management-tips-teens
This is the online presence for the Brooklyn Public Library,
   which is dedicated to educating families and teens in New
   York City, especially those in strained economic situations.

Caring for Kids
Canadian Paediatric Society
2305 St. Laurent Blvd., Suite 100
Ottawa, ON K1G 4J8
Canada
613-526-9397
http://www.caringforkids.cps.ca

This Canadian website has information for parents by
pediatricians.

Teenmentalhealth.org

5850 University Ave. PO Box 9700

Halifax, NS B3K 6R8

Canada

902-470-6598

http://teenmentalhealth.org

This website is dedicated to using scientific research to develop
application-ready training programs, publications, tools,
and resources to better understand and explore mental
health issues for teens.

WEBSITES

Because of the changing nature of internet links, Rosen Publishing has
developed an online list of websites related to the subject of this book.
This site is updated regularly. Please use this link to access the list:

http://www.rosenlinks.com/BYBS/time

FOR FURTHER READING

Allen, David. *Getting Things Done: The Art of Stress-Free Productivity*. New York, NY: Penguin Books, 2003.

Barnes, Emilie. *More Hours in My Day*. Eugene, OR: Harvest House, 2002.

Bennett, Arnold. *How to Live on 24 Hours a Day*. Hyattsville, MD: Shambling Gate Press, 2001.

Covey, Stephen R., A. Roger Merrill, and Rebecca R. Merrill. *First Things First*. New York, NY: Simon & Schuster, 1994.

Eisenberg, Ronni, and Kate Kelly. *The Overwhelmed Person's Guide to Time Management*. New York, NY: Plume, 1997.

Emmett, Rita. *The Procrastinator's Handbook: Mastering the Art of Doing It Now*. New York, NY: Walker & Company, 2000.

Fiore, Neil. *The Now Habit*. New York, NY: Tarcher, 2002.

Hindel, Tim, and Robert Heller. *Essential Managers: Managing Meetings*. New York, NY: DK Publishing, 1999.

Kennedy, Dan. *No B.S. Time Management for Entrepreneurs: The Ultimate No Holds Barred, Kick Butt, Take No Prisoners Guide to Time Productivity and Sanity*. Dallas, TX: Entrepreneur Press, 2004.

MacKenzie, R. Alec .*The Time Trap: The Classic Book on Time Management*. New York, NY: American Management Association, 1997.

Merrill, A. *Life Matters: Creating a Dynamic Balance of Work, Family, Time and Money*. Whitby, ON, Canada: McGraw-Hill, 2004.

Morgenstern, Julie. *Time Management from the Inside Out: The Foolproof System of Taking Control of Your Schedule and Your Life.* New York, NY: Henry Holt & Company, 2000.

Nakone, Lanna. *Organizing for Your Brain Type: Finding Your Own Solution to Managing Time, Paper, and Stuff.* New York, NY: St. Martin's Press, 2005.

Roesch, Roberta. *Time Management for Busy People.* New York, NY: McGraw-Hill, 1998.

Reno, Dawn E. *The Unofficial Guide to Managing Time.* New York, NY: John Wiley & Sons, 2000.

Silber, Lee. *Time Management for the Creative Person: Right-brain Strategies for Stopping Procrastination, Getting Control of the Clock and Calendar, and Freeing Up Your Time, and Your Life.* New York, NY: Three Rivers Press, 1998.

Staubus, Martin. *Time Management: Increase Your Personal Productivity and Effectiveness.* Boston, MA: Harvard Business School Press, 2005.

Tracey, Brian. *Time Power: A Proven System for Getting More Done in Less Time Than You Ever Thought Possible.* New York, NY: AMACOM, 2004.

Winston, Stephanie. *Organized Executive: A Program for Productivity: New Ways to Manage Time, Paper, People, and the Electronic Office.* New York, NY: Warner Books, 2001.

BIBLIOGRAPHY

The studies and papers referred to in this book are as follows:

Data Warehousing Institute Study, 2002.

Doherty, William J., and Barbara Z. Carlson. *Putting Family First: Successful Strategies for Reclaiming Family Life in a Hurry-up World.* New York, NY: Henry Holt, 2002.

McCown, W.G., and R. Roberts. "A Study of Academic and Work-Related Dysfunctioning Relevant to the College Version of an Indirect Measure of Impulsive Behavior." Integra Technical Paper 94–98, Radnor, 1984.

Moses, Barbara. *Career Intelligence: The New Rules for Work and Life Success.* ON, Canada: Stoddart, 1997.

Mosvick, R., and R. Nelson. *We've Got to Start Meeting Like This!* Glenview, IL: Scott Foresman, 1987.

Romano, Nicholas C., and Jay F. Nunamaker. "Meeting Analysis: Findings from Research and Practice." 34th Hawaii International Conference on System Sciences, 2001.

Solomon, L.J., and E.D. Rothblum, "Academic Procrastination: Frequency and Cognitivebehavioral Correlates." *Journal of Counseling Psychology*, 31: 504–510, 1984.

University of California Berkeley Study, 2002.

Waddington, P. *Dying for Information.* London, UK: Reuters Business Information, 1996.

INDEX

ABOUT THE AUTHOR

Lucy MacDonald is a Quebec-based motivational speaker with an academic background in psychology and counselling. Her clients include Pfizer Canada and McGill University.